AF323104

THE WORLD OF THE DIAMOND

THE WORLD OF THE DIAMOND

Isaac Pollak

Foreword by
ISIDORE LIPSCHUTZ
Former President
Belgian Diamond Manufacturers Association

An Exposition-Banner Book

Exposition Press   *Hicksville, New York*

Kind acknowledgment is made to Chilton Book Company, Radnor, Pennsylvania, for the use of material from *Diamonds*, by Eric Bruton, © 1971.

FIRST EDITION
© 1975 by Isaac Pollak

First printing, 1975
Second printing, 1979

Inquiries should be addressed to
Exposition Press, Inc.,
900 South Oyster Bay Road, Hicksville, N.Y. 11801

Library of Congress Catalog Card Number: 74-80687

ISBN 0-682-48006-1

Printed in the United States of America

To
My Parents
*Who have been a tremendous inspiration
and continuous influence on all my activities*

*We live with other men, and to other men,
not exclusively with, or to ourselves.
We have no intercourse with others that
does not tell on them, as they are all
the while influencing us.*
AUTHOR UNKNOWN

Contents

Foreword

Here is a young author who has taken upon himself a rather difficult assignment: to describe and comment on everything concerning the best-known and most appreciated precious stone civilized humanity has ever known. Everything is in the book: origin, mining, technology, the diamond's various uses, the pleasures it has given to millions, the joy and happiness it has created for uncounted human beings, the tragedies its possession has caused, the history of the most famous and biggest diamonds, the prosperity the diamond has created in its countries of origin, in those countries where it is converted into brilliant gems, and in those where it is used in hundreds of industrial applications, etc.

Nothing was omitted from this complete study, and the curious and interested reader who wants to enlarge his knowledge about the diamond will find here the answer to all possible questions.

ISIDORE LIPSCHUTZ
Former President,
Belgian Diamond Manufacturers
Association,
International Federation of
Diamond Organizations

Preface

Diamonds are a unique product. There is nothing else in the world to compare with a gemstone that warrants its name. The process that is involved in the formation of a diamond far beneath the earth's surface; the mining of the rough crystals; the intricate manufacturing and finishing process; and the marketplace where it is sold as a gem in a ring, brooch, or tie tack are processes that are fascinating and often complex.

Presenting this product to the public carries a responsibility involving both science and art. The scientific aspect involves the actual process of the diamond from mine to customer; the art encompasses the ability of communicating to the public the actual privilege of ownership. This does not imply that diamonds are pretentious. Rather, the potential diamond customer must realize that no matter what the size of the stone, the glimmering brilliance transmits far more than just beauty. Diamond—the mineral as well as the gemstone—has quality; not only quality of *substance*, however, but quality of *being*. These are attributes which cannot be communicated to a potential purchaser except through a thorough knowledge of the product.

The content of this book will catch the imagination of all readers interested in the most fascinating of all precious gems: the diamond. Its purpose is to provide a wealth of knowledge on an extremely exciting and involved topic. Special information on the retailing and marketing of diamonds is included in the Appendix.

When a diamond is studied for what it truly is, it becomes something more than a mere product. Upon completion of this book, it will become evident why the ancients believed diamonds actually had life; why some believed that the soul was purified after mortal death by becoming part of a diamond.

History, murder, tragedy, and love are all a part of the story of the diamond. In addition to these romantic concepts, the details of bringing diamonds from the ground to the consumer will be discussed. They are intricate and involved, but because they provide a vital understanding of the product, they are worth knowing. These precious gems are the end result of what began ages ago in the bowels of prehistoric volcanoes.

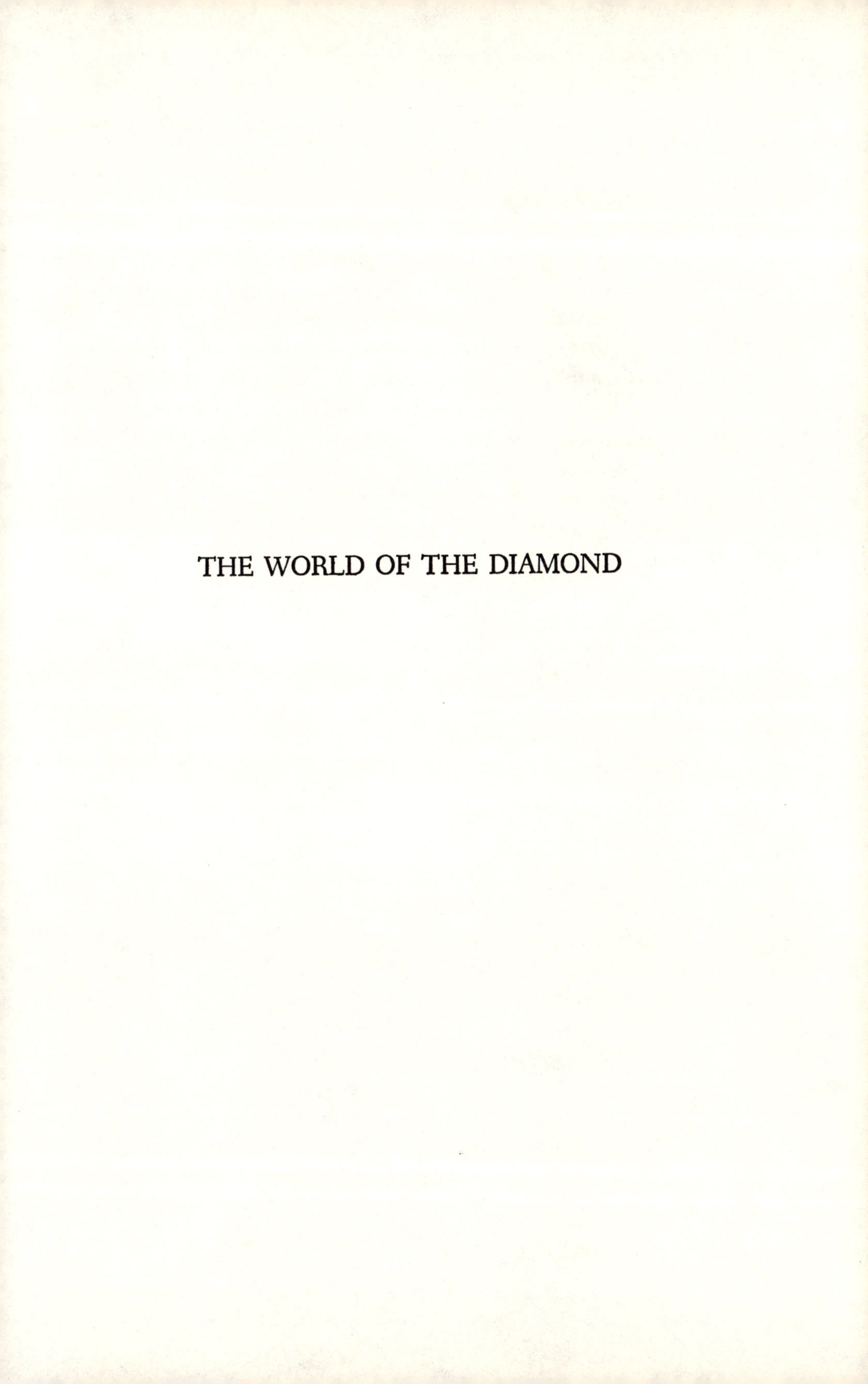

THE WORLD OF THE DIAMOND

CHAPTER I

Legend, Lore, Love:
The Romance of Diamonds

THE HISTORY OF THE DIAMOND is one of pure passion; a unique combination of tragedy, adventure, glamour, and mute testimony of torridly tempestuous times. Some of the stories that surround gems are filled with as much horror as a compilation of Edgar Allen Poe at his most depressed; some hold as much tenderness and love as Elizabeth Barrett Browning in her highest state of ecstasy.

The head of a ruler's friend is thrown into boiling oil; tragic deaths of children occur; insanity exists; trickery and megalomania by power-hungry moguls and emperors prevail; these are some of the passions that surround those silent gems that now repose softly amid the pompous surroundings of the world's great museums.

Diamonds have adorned the throats of the world's greatest ladies; they have been worn during ceremonies honoring history's great people; they have been the subjects of legends and myths as well as facts of history; they are themes to popular songs and have given glamour to those who could afford them.

And it is this fabric of fact, fantasy, and flair that has given them their reputation as the world's greatest gems, and maybe given them the "life" that has carried them down through the centuries to be gazed at today through glass enclosures, heavily guarded by armed men, by giggling girls, growing boys, the successful, the near-successful, and the unsuccessful.

In the Tower of London rests the famed Koh-i-Noor; the Hope permanently radiates its soft glow from a case in the Smithsonian Institution in Washington, D.C.; the Regent can be seen by anyone wishing to take the trouble to go to the Louvre; and the Kremlin houses the Orloff. From time to time they leave the confines of the museums and trek across oceans and continents to be paraded before the public.

Those who have but a passing knowledge of their history, stare in wonderment at this shimmering chunk of highly-finished carbon, which, were it able to talk, would keep them spellbound for hours with its own peculiar and fascinating story.

The Koh-i-Noor, reputed to have been found near the Godaveri River in India, was famous even in 1304. The Rajahs of what was then Malwa held it sacred until it fell into the clutches of the invading Moguls. Sultan Baber, founder of the Mogul Empire in India, became its possessor. In his diary of May, 1526, he mentioned a famous diamond so valuable that it would pay "half the expenses of the world." It weighed, he claimed, about two hundred carats.

When Jean Baptiste Tavernier traveled to India in the seventeenth century, he visited Aurangzeb, the last of the great Moguls and a descendant of Baber. Aurangzeb had imprisoned his father, successfully subdued his ambitious brothers, and wore an iron claw strapped to one arm which he used as a weapon to disembowel his enemies. His favorite name for himself was "Alamgir," the "grasper of the universe." He died in his bed at the age of eighty-nine as his suffering subjects, steeped in poverty and slavery, bordered on revolt.

Among the diamonds Aurangzeb showed Tavernier was a huge stone, rose-cut, cleaved, and faceted by the Venetian cutter Hortensio Borgia. It later became known as the Great Mogul and, according to Tavernier, weighed two hundred and eighty carats and had come from a rough stone once weighing nine hundred carats.

In 1739 Nadir Shah of Persia invaded India, captured Delhi, and went on a systematic search for the Mogul's great diamonds. Legend or fact, the story makes interesting reading, because he learned through a member of the vanquished Mogul's harem the secret of the great diamond's hiding place—the emperor's turban.

Since it wasn't quite proper, even then, to force a showdown with an enemy leader personally over such an issue, Nadir Shah took advantage of an old Oriental tradition and invited the emperor to a banquet honoring the Persian victory. There he suggested the two rulers exchange turbans, executing the exchange even as he proposed it. Quickly he went back to his tent, unrolled the silk and found a single, huge stone. As it fell into line with his fevered gaze, he is said to have murmured, "Koh-i-Noor!" and the "Mountain of Light" was named.

Nadir later was assassinated; the stone went to his son who was tortured to death for he would not give it up. From there it went to a friend of the Shah's offspring who himself endured a few select tortures, including having his head boiled in oil.

Lost with the kingdom, it next went to the Afghans and then to the Sikhs. When Lahore was annexed to British India in 1849, its treasury yielded the Koh-i-Noor which was seized by the British as reparations from the Sikhs. It was presented to Queen Victoria in 1850 who wasn't exactly fascinated by it, despite the ardor of its former owners. People who saw it on display termed it dull, lacking fire; the British had been duped, they said, and so the Queen had it recut in hopes of giving it more fire, more life, more brilliance. Thirty-eight days later—after the pomp and circumstance of a state event which accompanied a very bad cutting job—the Mountain of Light lost seventy-eight carats in weight and gained almost nothing in brilliance. At last, in 1911, it was given a place of respect and placed as the central ornament in the crown of Queen Mary.

Controversy surrounds the gem; some say it is not the Great Mogul that Tavernier observed on his trip to India; they say that stone was lost. Today it is generally accepted to be the Great Mogul, but a mutilated, badly cut version of that oldest diamond known to man.

Then there is the Orloff, a gem weighing just under two hundred carats, and shaped like half an egg. Its history is traced to an idol of the god Sri-Ranga in a tiny village temple some two hundred miles above the southern tip of India. Disguised as a Brahmin, a French grenadier (a deserter from the Indian foreign legion) managed to steal the diamond from one of the eyes of the idol, wresting it from the socket as a storm raged outside. He sold it in Madras to a British sea captain for two thousand pounds, and the captain sold it in England for six times that sum.

Somehow, it came into the possession of a Persian jeweler named Khojeh who took it to Amsterdam and, in 1774, convinced Prince Orloff to buy it as a gift for his queen, Catherine the Great of Russia.

Later, Catherine had it mounted atop the double eagle in her imperial sceptre after ousting Orloff and his brothers from her bed and court. She preferred gems to gentlemen and is reputed to have worn 2,536 diamonds just in her crown.

The history of the magnificent blue Hope diamond is somewhat different; the Hope holds a place in American lore and is tied to tragedy, sorrow, madness, and possessiveness.

Among the gems shown to Louis XIV by Tavernier in 1668, was a blue diamond weighing 122.50 carats. Even then it carried a legend of bringing misfortune to its owner and was a subject of fear to one of Louis' mistresses, the Marquise de Montespan.

Marie Antoinette wore it when Louis XVI inherited the beautiful blue, after it had been recut Indian style into the form of a heart. During the Revolution, it was carted away in a jewel theft and never seen again.

More than likely, the blue heart was sold in Spain and cut into three smaller stones. A Goya portrait of Queen Maria Luisa of Spain shows her wearing what apparently was her share of the French Blue. It is this stone, weighing 44.50 carats of rounded oval, which now reposes in the Smithsonian. It took awhile to reach the American capital, however.

It was offered for sale in London in 1830 and purchased by Henry Philip Hope, a wealthy banker, for $90,000. It stayed in the Hope family until the turn of the century. Once again it became the center of tragedy.

Keep in mind that Louis XIV died a miserable death from smallpox, and Louis XVI and Marie Antoinette underwent the guillotine before Hope ever came into ownership of the blue. Hope died a bachelor and willed the stone to a nephew who, in turn, willed it to a grandson. The grandson's wife left him for another man and the last of the Hopes went bankrupt, selling the stone to a jeweler.

During the next few years it changed owners rather rapidly, landing in the hands of a Follies' star who wore it and was murdered by her lover. A Greek broker bought it and fell from a cliff along with his wife and children. The Sultan of Turkey had to sell it when he found himself facing revolution.

It was Pierre Cartier, a French jeweler, who purchased the stone and sold it to Mr. and Mrs. Edward B. McLean of Washington, D.C., he the son of a millionaire publisher (the *Washington Post*), and she the daughter of a wealthy miner. They paid $154,000 for it.

Mrs. McLean loved the Hope.

But her son was killed in a car wreck; her daughter died of an overdose of sleeping pills; her husband suffered a nervous breakdown and died in a mental hospital.

After Mrs. McLean died in 1947, the Hope was sold to Harry Winston, along with other McLean jewels, for more than one million dollars. Winston mailed it to the Smithsonian in November of 1958, shelling out $145 in stamps to insure the gem for one million dollars.

The eighteenth century was just about one year old when a slave, working the Parteal mines on the Kistna River in India, found something for which he was willing to risk his life—a 410-carat rough diamond. He decided to smuggle it out of the mine rather than take the prize which would have been his for the discovery.

This was the first of several incidents of tragedy that surrounded the stone that came to be known as the Regent diamond.

The slave slashed a hole in his leg, stuffed the crystal into the wound, wrapped it in bandages, and headed for the coast. There he found a ship's captain who offered him an escape to freedom for a fifty-fifty cut on the value of the diamond.

Once at sea, the captain stole the stone from the slave, pushed the luckless man overboard, located a diamond merchant in the Orient after he reached shore, and was one thousand pounds richer for his trouble.

The captain apparently was not an emotionally stable individual, and he squandered the money and wound up at the end of a rope he had managed to rig for his own neck.

Now the stone was in the possession of the merchant, a man named Jamchaud, who had only slight success with it. First he had a hard time selling the stone because of its size and also because it was stolen property.

Thomas Pitt, the British-appointed governor of Fort St. George near Madras, was not wealthy, but he invited Jamchaud to Madras as his guest to see some of the gems the merchant had for sale. Pitt wasn't about to pay the eighty-five-thousand-pound price Jamchaud was asking for the big stone, and after several months of haggling, he managed to pressure the merchant down to 20,400 pounds.

When Pitt returned to England, however, he had a tough time convincing anyone he had come by the stone legally and repeatedly was forced to the defensive in answering attacks on his story of the purchase. However, he went ahead and had it cut to a brilliant of 140.50 carats, which cost him another twenty-five thousand pounds. Pitt managed to retrieve the dust which sold for about eight thousand pounds, then cut the extra pieces into rose cuts which were bought by Peter the Great of Russia. When that phase of the possession by Pitt was completed, the owner had made quite a profit out of the venture, but he still was unable to sell the big stone. He had a morbid fear of being robbed and murdered as the owner of the gem, so he disguised himself whenever he carried it, never slept in the same house more than two successive nights, and refused to show the stone or even acknowledge that he carried it if he were recognized by someone.

But in 1717—sixteen years after it had been found in its rough massiveness by the unfortunate slave—Pitt sold what was then called the Pitt diamond for 135,000 pounds to the Duke of Orleans, then the Regent of France.

Pitt, from whose family came the famed William Pitt (after whom Pittsburgh was named), never managed to clear his name of the scandal that continually dogged him to his grave.

Now the Regent's history takes on additional flavor—this time of royal vintage. In the royal inventory of the French court, the stone was valued at 480,000 pounds, or nearly $2.5 million. It was the crown's most valuable gem.

Then, in 1792, when Louis XVI and Marie Antoinette were imprisoned, the Regent was placed in the Garde Meuble along with the other jewels of royalty. There it was stolen again, but immediately recovered from a ditch in Paris.

The Ministry of France came into possession of the Regent and used it for collateral on loans. By the time Napoleon ruled France, the country was free of debt, and the new ruler had it set in the hilt of the sword he carried during his coronation ceremony as emperor of France. When Napoleon went into exile, his wife, Marie Louise, pried it from the sword, took it home to Austria with her, and was forced to send it back by her somewhat more virtuous father.

In 1887 the crown jewels were put up for auction, but the diadem was retained and placed in a case in the Louvre where it rests today—a quiet end for a stormy stone.

Other stories of other gems are almost as plentiful as the people who have worn them over the centuries. Many of the accounts involve much the same trickery, suspense, plotting and intrigue, tragedy, sorrow, and death that plagued the gems already described.

It is against this type of legendary and factual backdrop that diamonds have become the lore-filled gem of substance that women the world over long to possess, and when in possession, wear with a pride no other adornment can match.

Although the United States certainly has had its social "royalty," whose penchant for diamonds easily matches many of Europe's monarchs, it took a good many years for this nation to evolve into a jewelry-wearing populace. So much of the early history of the United States is concerned with settling land and forging cities and towns from frontiers, that it is easy to see how the people were more concerned with existing than with the luxuries of life such as diamonds.

Even at that time there were jewelers and jewelry among the early eighteenth-century colonists; Paul Revere and his family were among the most notable. They were French-born gold and silversmiths. Even though they lived among the austere Puritans who disdained wedding bands as pagan and ostentatious, the Reveres sold gold rings to other colonists and manufactured silver spoons and other items of precious metals.

This marked the beginning of the world of fashion in America; a slow start, perhaps, but nevertheless a start. There were at least two periods of peak interest in gems, with wars in between, and families of prominence dominating the social scene and, consequently, the gem display of their generations.

One of the early pacesetters of American jewelry fashion was a President's wife, Dolley Madison. Even during the blockade of 1812, the wife of President James Madison managed to have her clothes and jewels arrive successfully from Paris. At White House receptions she was at her best in a brilliant diamond crescent.

A party-giver of renowned capacity, Mrs. Madison was followed as the nation's first lady until President John Tyler's daughter-in-law, Priscilla, began presiding over White House social life in satins, silks, and more diamonds.

Since America has no monarchy and never did, the nation depended on its Presidents' wives to furnish the pace in fashion. Priscilla Tyler, in bringing her daughter out at the White House, dressed the child as Queen Titania with a wand in one hand and a diamond on her forehead to receive Washington's elite and near elite. When the widowed President married Julia Gardiner, the beautiful "Rose of Long Island" as she was known to reporters, the White House took on the appearance of a court, with Mrs. Tyler surrounded by twelve maids of honor, receiving guests on a raised platform, a headdress resembling a crown on her hair during the day, and a tiara of diamonds at night-time affairs.

During this time, a store on lower Broadway in New York accidentally got into the jewelry business and evolved into the New World's version of Paris at its most brilliant. It was called Tiffany and Young and boasted of its unique and fancy yard goods from France, England, and the Far East. During a visit to Paris, John Young learned a group of royalists wished to sell their diamonds. He cabled Tiffany and the latter cabled back to get all he could, bring it home, and they'd sell it. One hundred years later Tiffany's adorned New York's Fifth Avenue as a great jewelry business—the nation's bright light of gem retailing.

The gold rush of the late 1840's in California helped establish a jewelry trade in the United States that nearly came to a standstill during the Civil War. President Lincoln's wife, Mary Todd, was fond of both clothes and jewelry, even to the point of slitting her gloves to reveal her rings. But during the war a single-strand necklace, a pair of matching gold bracelets, jeweled combs, a gold wedding band, and a "keeper ring" of sparks was acceptable for a socialite's jeweled display in public.

When the war ended, another fashion buildup occurred in society which led into the Gay Nineties and a profusion of blatant extravagance in jewelry of every imaginable form, especially diamonds. The industrial revolution was well underway, the new rich were coming to power in America, and palatial homes with ocean-going yachts and such ostentatious displays as William H. Vanderbilt's block-long Fifth Avenue brownstone mansion, built at a cost of three million dollars, became the American way—at least for the wealthy few.

Typical of the more adventuresome Americans was "Diamond Jim Brady," perhaps the greatest diamond collector of modern days, who had a different set of monogrammed jewelry for each day of the month. He wore diamonds one day, emeralds the next, turquoise, rubies, sapphires, and an almost gaudy transportation set studded with 2,548 diamonds set into a railroad car, tank car, coal car, and even a caboose.

It has been estimated that Brady owned more than 20,000 diamonds and sometimes wore as much as $25,000 worth on a single day.

Diamonds became sufficiently fashionable. The social maxim (which Brady helped perpetrate) that diamonds were not to be worn by socially-conscious people in the daytime, was violated by the rich as well as the near rich.

The story goes that when a young matron wore her diamond brooch to a luncheon, she was told by a slightly pompous dowager that the brooch was out of place at such an occasion.

"I thought so, too, until I got it," was the tart reply.

Mrs. Evelyn Walsh McLean wore her Hope diamond day and night. Bailey's Beach was the "in" swimming place in those days and Mrs. McLean wore the gem even while she swam. This made the presence of a detective necessary, who was by her side at all times as she paddled in the water.

In the three decades before the turn of the century, however, the real diamond display came at night. One popular display was a pearl dog collar which soon gave way in fashion to the diamond dog collar and then later to bibs of diamonds.

Consuelo Vanderbilt began the trend, wearing on her young, slim neck a dog collar with nineteen rows of pearls. Since few women had the graceful neckline of Miss Vanderbilt, it was understandable when the bib came into fashion. The bib was set in heavy gold—very elaborate and impressive—but it chafted the neck and was quite uncomfortable.

As the Gay Nineties came into full bloom, the jewelry business in America was setting a frantic pace.

Lillian Russell, a light opera star of the period, rivaled Mrs. Cornelius Vanderbilt for fashion attention, wearing as much as one million dollars in diamonds at one time. A photograph of opera star Geraldine Farrar, taken about 1895, shows her wearing a matched tiara and dog collar in diamonds and pearls, said to be equaled only by the gems of Mrs. Jay Gould. Miss Farrar wore her own jewels in her operatic roles, a practice similar to that of other prima donnas of the Metropolitan Opera in New York.

The tiara became the pinnacle of diamond fashion about this time. Some contained as many as a thousand gems and nearly all could be converted into other forms of jewelry. The center section, for example, could be broken off and used as a brooch, with side sections used as clips, bracelets, or pendants. Prices started at $25,000, and from that point you could pay up to any price conceivable.

These were lavish, tax-free days for America's rich; war-free for the most part, they were times of opulence, if not affluence. The wealthy never lacked an appropriate occasion on which to wear their diamonds. The opening of the opera in New York, Philadelphia, or Boston was the ideal occasion on which tiara owners could exercise their most blatant exhibitionist tendencies at will. During the fall, scores of elaborate private parties were held along Fifth Avenue; at Palm Beach in January; Saratoga Springs in May; Newport in July or August—parties with a hundred guests or more, each couple with a footman, and ten-course meals served on solid gold services. A woman could spend $250,000 just for one of these affairs, and many did.

And there were the "social rulers" of this late nineteenth-century American society as well. Mrs. William Backhouse Astor, that is, *the* Mrs. Astor, and *the* Mrs. Cornelius Vanderbilt vied for the honor. Mrs. Astor was once described by a friend as "a walking chandelier." She kept two social secretaries, Ward McAllister and Harry Lehr, and was supported by a tax-free eighty million dollars earned by her husband who was almost never around. She ruled undaunted for four decades, and only when she retreated into a make-believe party world of her own did the gilded age of publicly displayed wanton wealth enter its slow decline. When 1900 dawned, it was clear that the social age of this form of opulence was over. The "Roaring Twenties" and, to a lesser extent, the "Fabulous Fifties" tried to recapture some of the glitter, but they never came close.

During the years prior to World War I, Europe took over the world of fashion. In 1901, austere and tiny Queen Victoria died, and the handsome Edward VII and his Danish-born Queen Alexandra assumed the British throne.

They immediately set a pace for luxury that even an American tycoon had difficulty matching.

Platinum, discovered in Russia shortly before the nineteenth century closed, began to replace gold as the setting for diamonds. It was lighter, more easily worked, and gave added glitter to diamonds because of the background of whiteness provided by the metal.

America, in what may have been an unconscious attempt to emulate the beautiful new British queen, evolved their own special "princess"—Alice Roosevelt, the lovely daughter of President Teddy Roosevelt. She was sufficiently bright, flamboyant, and intelligent to make news on her own. Since no one could decide how she should be ranked, she was not permitted to attend the coronation of Edward VII, but took a series of trips to Puerto Rico, New Orleans, the St. Louis World's Fair and, in 1905, went to Japan where she was presented to the royal family and the old Empress Dowager of China.

A companion on the trip was Nicholas Longworth, a native of Ohio, later Speaker of the U.S. House of Representatives. He married Miss Roosevelt two years later in a White House ceremony that glittered around the world. Among the wedding gifts was a $25,000 pearl necklace with a diamond clasp, a chest of Chinese silks, a French tapestry, antique Spanish jewelry, and a diamond and pearl pendant.

But the new Mrs. Longworth was more interested in politics than fashion and never seriously challenged Alexandra's reign as world fashion leader.

The war considerably slowed down traffic of European luxuries and America again contributed significantly to the fashion world, this time in a less ostentatious manner.

Special rings for specific occasions were introduced by

Jaccard's of Kansas City: dinner rings, lunch rings, and reception rings, later known as cocktail rings.

When the wartime economy demanded the return of all the gold to the government, platinum took on new significance as the metal used as a setting for jewelry.

Following the war, dowager jewelry lost its appeal as more and more people began demanding jewels for fashion. In Texas, where oil discoveries began making families wealthy, some men even began carrying diamonds loose in their pockets.

The next major phase of America's fashion influence began with the moving picture business. This industry soon dominated all that was said, worn, and practiced as social custom. The stars that made Hollywood the legendary city collected the largest homes, the finest furs, and the most luxurious diamonds—and they made the swimming pool a new status symbol.

Merle Oberon became known for her twenty-seven diamond bracelets, five diamond necklaces, and three diamond roses, plus a necklace of diamonds and emeralds with matching earrings, once owned by Napoleon Bonapart.

The stars who brought beauty and a new display of sensuousness to American life had no rules for wearing jewels; they wore them with bathing suits, slacks, negligees, on their ankles, and sometimes on their toes.

An interesting fact in diamond history occurred in the 1930's when the depression was at its worst. Old Philadelphia families were forced to bring heirloom jewelry out of hiding and cash it in for money. It was in the East where the post Civil War fortunes had been made, but it was in the West where the jewelry which had become part of those fortunes was sent as America crawled out from under economic hardship. Hollywood was screaming for diamonds, and Philadelphia and other cities gave them up for the now socially dominant movie queens and princesses.

In 1943 worldwide diamond sales reached seventy-eight million dollars. Most of this was in engagement rings. Macy's in New York became a diamond brokerage house where gems could be bought, sold, advertised, and traded.

During World War II the fashion involved jewelry, but as the war ended, sentimentality took over and the diamond engagement ring and diamond-set wedding band reached full prominence.

But the economic upheaval in Europe, set off by two world wars, took its toll in family jewelry as estates were brought under the auctioneer's hammer and much of what had been in European families for generations passed into American hands. Fashion etiquette became less and less meaningful. This was best illustrated when Elizabeth Taylor wore her diamonds with a gingham dress, incurring the wrath of social etiquette "authorities." Miss Taylor merely laughed.

Junk jewelry and poor imitations of the real thing came into being and adorned the garb of anyone wishing to appear "fashionable."

America's latest fling into semi-royalty and a Camelot-like preoccupance with the glitter of gems came in the early 1960's, when John F. Kennedy and his fashionable and beautiful wife Jacqueline set a new pace in the White House. Both the President and First Lady came from established, wealthy families, and although Mrs. Kennedy was reluctant to discuss her diamonds, it was known that she owned and wore at least a dozen pieces of importance.

For the discussion on lore, legend, and love to be complete, it must include the sentimentality and romance attached to a bride's ring and to the gems given wives and mistresses of wealthy men over the ages.

The ring—a symbol of love and protection—has roots that go deep into the history and even prehistory of our world. In nearly every archaeological discovery, the ring, or at least the circle, is found to have played an important part in the life of the civilization under study. It may have been ivory, as in Africa; iron, as in Italy; even bone, leather and, in earlier periods, grass. But gold, brass, iron, copper, silver, and platinum formed the ring that was used on ankles, in the nose, around the head, through the ear and on the finger. These early rings bore religious overtones, as they were used to keep the soul of the individual intact.

An interesting thread of history concerns the "ring finger," or the third finger of the left hand. The Egyptians, master embalmers and lords of a huge portion of the earth at the height of their dominance, also possessed a romantic streak and decided that a "vein of love" ran from the heart, directly to the tip of the third finger of the left hand. Pledges between lovers were made by extending this finger toward the partner's "love finger" until they touched, then the seal of the ring was put into place. The custom was adopted by the Greeks and Romans, even though other fingers, even the thumbs, were used to hold rings for various reasons.

The religious implication of rings was evident in sixteenth-century betrothal, or wedding bands. They were called "gimmals" or twins, and each lover wore two, interlocked with the Latin inscription *Quod Deus conjunxit homo non separet*, spread across all four rings. The inscription is translated into the well-known words used in nearly all wedding ceremonies: "What God has joined together, let no man separate."

Rings have signified many things to many people. For example, the ancient Romans wore *iron* rings to signify mourning if they were poor, and *gold* if they were rich.

Engraved rings, studded with gems or adorned with cameos, were found in the ashes at Pompeii; amber was well known and a favorite for engraving. The cheapest rings were of glass, ivory, jet, and stone; pearls and rubies set in gold were worn on the fingers of the rich.

Romans and Hebrews both used wedding rings but with a slight difference; when a Roman of the freeman or noble class desired to marry a particular woman, he went to her father or guardian and gained permission. Then, in the presence of bride and bridegroom, her parents and his, a marriage agreement was drawn up in which possessions were listed which she would bring into the new home and those he would contribute to the union. When the pact was sealed, the groom would present a ring to the bride as a bond of the agreement.

Early Hebrews married under a canopy, much as Orthodox Jews do today; this signified both husband and wife had entered a world of their own. A ring was used during the ceremony but it was not worn by the wife until after the ceremony was over. Early Christians adopted the custom, adding a blessing to the use of the wedding band and choosing the third finger on the left hand as the marriage finger.

Jewish wedding rings were inscribed in various ways, most quite elaborately, and they often bore the words, *Mazel Tov,* or, "Good Luck."

Although the durability of a ring's substance signified the durability of the relationship, there is a practical side to it all as well. The ring came to signify the man's dependability, and his responsibility for the woman and the children she bore into the relationship.

There is a psychological sidelight to the decline and eventual decadence to the Roman Empire which involves rings. As decadence grew, so did the weight and durability of rings, as if to lend to the wearer an added sense of security in the face of the obvious decline of the empire and the feeling of inward fear this realization would have brought had the emotion been allowed to surface.

The first diamond ring known to be given as a love pledge involves a story of incest. Agrippa, appointed king of the Jews by the Roman emperor Caligula, fell in love with his sister. In binding their relationship, he pledged his fidelity with the gift of a diamond ring. When the sister, Berenice, left him for another man (Titus), Agrippa tore the ring from her hand and placed it in public view as a symbol of her disgrace in breaking the pledge.

This was enough to ruin the diamond's reputation as a love band for some time following the incident.

During the Renaissance there was a lack of diamonds available to the general population. As the power of the Christian Church deepened and spread across Europe, there were legal prohibitions against the wearing of jewelry by men other than clergy or noblemen. Trade with infidels who handled diamonds also was forbidden. During the early years of the Middle Ages, there was some use of diamond to ward off devils, but as scientific curiosity evolved to scientific discovery in later generations, the talismanic use of diamond gave way to more ornamental use.

In the reign of Charles VII of France, financier Jacques Coeur became known for displaying cut diamonds, and the trend evolved into the use of diamonds as love gems. By 1477 the court counsel of the Archduke Maximilian of Germany ordered Coeur to prepare two rings for his marriage to Mary of Burgundy. One of the rings, set with a diamond, was to be used as an engagement ring, and the other, a gold band, would be the wedding ring.

Other gems were used in connection with marriage in the sixteenth century. Martin Luther chose a ruby ring when he broke his vows of celibacy as a priest to marry a nun. The Tudors of England placed a ruby in the coronation ring to signify the divine marriage of State and Church. However, the diamond also found a place as the symbolic love gem among the Tudors who gave away diamond rings as love and loyalty pledges in a manner which can best be described as extravagant.

The infamous Henry VIII of England recklessly appropriated diamonds to the nobles who supported him in his many marriages, divorces, and executions. In his gem room in the palace, or so he boasted, he possessed a diamond as big as a walnut. His fingers underwent nightly fatigue from the many rings he wore, and he was the owner of as many diamonds as a good-sized meadow had flowers in spring—or so it seemed.

Although diamond mines continued to open up during the eighteenth and nineteenth centuries, diamonds remained the possessions of the wealthy until after World War I.

It was in the period of the 1920's that the diamond engagement ring began coming into its own as a possession to be cherished for the love it symbolized. The engagement ring did not need a large stone to be prized as the symbol of a love relationship. On the contrary, most diamond rings given since that time have included comparatively small gems. A fraction of a carat, set into white or yellow gold, was sufficient to bring the little feminine cries of ecstasy associated with a proposal of marriage.

And a ritual has evolved around the engagement ring. Often, couples shop together, and the man permits the woman to more or less choose a ring within a certain price range. Perhaps she will choose several stones and let the man make the final selection later. Or the man may purchase what he can afford, then propose, and present the engagement ring at that time. However, choosing the latter option, the man would have to be quite certain he wouldn't be turned down. Once accepted, the engagement ring symbolized the future betrothal of the young lady. It wasn't final, by any means, but in the large majority of cases, it was sufficient to keep her faithful and send her into frantic preparations for the wedding.

The American economy was especially suited to the purchase of an engagement ring and matching wedding band. With the entry of easy credit into the economic system, a young man could purchase the rings at a price beyond his immediate means, then take several months to pay for them. As a consequence, the engagement ring would become the first gift of value to his fiancée.

Surrounding this ritual, a great amount of sentimentality has grown. Movies, advertisements, the thrill of receiving a gift of durability and value—all went into the legendary giving of diamonds for love. And the legend went deep.

When Patrick Kennedy, the baby son of President and Mrs. John F. Kennedy, died, they had placed a gold St. Christopher's medal into the coffin—a medal Jacqueline had given Jack when they became engaged. After the President was assassinated in November of 1963, his widow stood alone beside his coffin. Then she did something that immediately became known around the world and even became part of the eulogies given the slain President. She took her wedding ring and placed it upon the finger of her dead husband. "And she took a ring, and placed it on his hand . . ." So went the eulogy.

Late that night, before the coffin was taken to burial, she asked Kenneth O'Donnell, a friend of her husband's, if she had done the right thing. "Now I have nothing left," she explained.

O'Donnell went to the hospital, retrieved the ring, and gave it back to her. She murmured her thanks and slipped it back on her finger.

Such is the stuff legends are made of. The facts of love and the incidents that surround that love. It's a circle of faith, of love, of an abiding quality to life that only a diamond can give.

Jackie Kennedy was not the first wife to take seriously that glittering symbol; she was one of millions. But as part of that historic and meaningful family of the loved and the loving, she symbolized to them all what love and diamonds are all about.

CHAPTER 2

Diamonds in History

THERE IS SLIGHT CONFUSION surrounding the origin of the word "diamond." In tracing the word's history, I have come upon two origins, one of which probably referred to other minerals but now applies to what is known today as diamond.

The word itself, "diamond," comes from the old French, "diamant." But diamant is derived from Latin and also from Greek. The Greeks had a word, "adamas," which means "unconquerable." However, adamas was the word for iron, or iron alloy, as far back as 800 B.C. Apparently lacking a word to apply to other substances as hard, or harder than iron, adamas was used to apply to what probably was the diamond.

It is believed that Ovid, writing in the second half of the first century B.C., was really referring to diamond when using the word "adamas."

Much of the history of diamond concerns legend and

myth. The writings of the Roman philosopher Pliny the Elder exemplies this. Pliny wrote, "These stones [diamonds] are tested upon the anvil, and will resist the blow to such an extent as to make the iron rebound and the very anvil split asunder . . . this invincible force which defies Nature's two most violent forces, iron and fire, can be broken by ram's blood. But it must be steeped in blood that is fresh and warm and, even so, many blows are needed . . ." In fact, he went so far as to claim diamond could even split the iron hammer in two. Pliny's writings on diamond were included in a volume of his *Natural History* devoted to precious stones.

Pliny wrote of a "Valley of Diamonds" a legend that persisted for centuries and, at times, involved such historical figures as Alexander the Great and Marco Polo. Alexander, during a campaign through India in about 350 B.C., was said to have plucked diamonds from a pit guarded by snakes. Supposedly, the gaze of the snakes had the power to kill a man. Alexander's soldiers, rather ingeniously, simply used mirrors so that the gaze of the snakes fell upon the snakes themselves. Carcasses of sheep were then thrown into the pit. The diamonds stuck to the fat of the butchered animals. Vultures, lured to the site by the fresh carrion, picked up the chunks of diamond-studded sheep fat and carried them to their roosts. The soldiers recovered the gems from nests and droppings.

Rather messy, but it makes for interesting mythology. The story apparently originated in the writings of the Bishop of Constantia, Cyprus (circa 315-403); it was later given new life by Marco Polo.

Professor Samuel Tolansky, an authority on diamonds, has proposed the idea that the Valley of Diamonds was advanced by Indian diamond merchants in Golconda, the trading center of that area of the world, to mask the actual source of the gems—the riverbeds in the surrounding countryside. Also, he advances the theory that the ram's or goat's blood legend may have been encouraged as a camouflage for the art of cleaving. Cleaving is the process by which a diamond may be split according to the grain of the stone.

Jerome Cardan, in 1501, writing on gemmology, classified all stones with brilliance as gems, but reserved the expression "precious stones" for those having brilliance coupled with rare, small dimensions. He stated that the diamond was distilled from gold and was among those precious stones possessing life, suffering illness, old age, and death.

This is an especially interesting part of the history of diamonds, because the "life" possessed by the stones produced spiritual powers which were incorporated into religious belief.

An example is Buddhism, where the soul of the dead, if impure, passed through a process of transmigration. The soul would take the form of an animal, plant, and even mineral, until it was purified and absorbed into the universal soul. Gemstones were included in this process. Consequently, gemstones had life, according to Buddhist belief. It was a belief which spread from ancient India through the East. It came to Egypt and to Greece and even to Europe in the Middle Ages, especially through the activities of alchemists.

Diamonds have been involved in medicine, possessing both poisonous and curative powers.

As a medicine, the diamond supposedly had the power to resist all poisons, but only through external application. When used internally, it was believed to be a poison in itself. Despite this contradiction, St. Hildegard, in the tenth century, believed that diamonds had healing abilities if they were held in the hand as the sign of the cross was made. Also, he held that the diamond could heal if taken to bed and warmed against the body. Additional healing abilities were attributed to the diamond, especially when fasting, if it was held in the mouth, breathed upon, or worn next to the skin. St. Hildegard also maintained that if a diamond was held in the mouth of a liar it would cure the individual's spiritual defects.

The Hindus believed that the power of a flawed diamond was poisonous, producing various illnesses and diseases: lameness, jaundice, pleurisy, and leprosy.

Diamond as poison has also been related to specific events in history. Emperor Frederick II (1194-1250) died by a fatal dose of powdered diamond, according to legend. Turkish Sultan Bejazet (1447-1512) allegedly was poisoned fatally by his son who mixed a large amount of pulverized diamond in the sultan's food. Catherine de Medici, the dominating wife of Henry II of France, is said to have died of powdered diamond in her food and drink in the mid-1600s. This became known as the *poudre de succession.* However, it is more than likely that arsenic was mixed with the powdered diamond in bringing about death.

Magical powers were attributed to precious stones in the seventeenth century when diamonds were equated with the sun, giving them astrological significance in the table of planets.

Another belief was that one's teeth would drop out if the gem were held in the mouth. Diamonds were said to repel the attacks of phantoms; give freedom from nightmares when worn in sleep; dispel fears when worn in battle; and give courage and other moral virtues in the process: If a house, orchard, or vineyard were touched at each corner with a diamond, the property supposedly would be protected from lightning, storms, and blight.

Some diamonds possessed the ability to glow in the dark after prolonged exposure to bright sunlight. It was this ability that produced so-called proof of a diamond's magic during Roman times and possibly even earlier.

As the credibility of the powers of the diamond waned in the Middle Ages, the stone's importance slipped—even as a gem to be worn for beautification. It was only when cutting and polishing techniques improved in later years that the diamond reclaimed its high place on the list of gems. By then, of course, the reasons for wearing the stone had changed considerably.

The evolution of diamond from talisman to jewel probably came about in India, where it was used first as a magical protection, then as a sign of rank and power. Although Romans wore diamonds set in gold rings as early as A.D. 100, they were worn for "protection" rather than for beauty.

About 1075, the Crown of St. Stephen, perhaps the earliest jeweled piece still in existence, was set with uncut diamonds. It also has become known as the Holy Crown of Hungary. But the existence of the crown completed the transition.

Mention of a diamond as jewelry, however, is not found until 1319, when a diamond necklace was reportedly worn by the French Queen Clemence, Hungarian wife of King Louis the Quarreler.

The Duke of Burgundy gave his mother a ruby brooch surrounded by diamonds and pearls in 1369, and in 1396, when King Richard II of England married Isabella of France (his second wife and only seven years old at the time), he gave her a collar of diamonds, rubies, and large pearls.

During the reign of Queen Elizabeth I, from 1558 to 1603, diamonds were beginning to take their place in romantic relationships. It became fashionable among the more wealthy to wear rings set with octahedral crystals of diamond. (These gave the appearance of two four-sided pyramids, joined at the bases, with the point of one of the four-sided pyramids to the front.) They became known as "scribbling rings," since they often were used to scribble love messages on glass windowpanes. It was said that the Virgin Queen and Sir Walter Raleigh would exchange love messages in rhyme on a windowpane.

Any history of diamonds must include those spectacular gems which have acquired the fame that has placed most of them in museums, or under the tightest security.

The "Koh-i-Noor," or Mountain of Light, was in the possession of the Rajahs of Malwa as early as 1304. It is believed to have been set by the Mogul emperors in the famous Peacock Throne as one of the eyes of the peacock. The other eye is said to have been the Akbar Shah diamond. It was taken by the Persian Shah when he invaded India in 1739 and later fell into the hands of the "Lion of Punjab" who took it in return for military help he never gave. Eventually, it was taken by the East India Company for protection against losses and presented to Queen Victoria of England in 1850. However, the queen was disappointed that the gem lacked fire, so she had it recut from its original 186-carat weight to an oval brilliant weighing 108.9 carats. This version of the historic stone may be seen today among the British Crown Jewels in the Tower of London when it is not being worn by the Queen Mother on state occasions as part of the circlet of her crown.

In 1701 the 410-carat Regent Diamond was found in India. It was the last discovery of that nation's big diamonds. It came to England and, after being recut, was resold to the Regent of France, who gave it its name. Marie Antoinette wore it and, on September 17, 1792, it was among the French Crown Jewels stolen during the early stages of the French Revolution. Most of the treasures were recovered but the Regent did not reappear until fifteen months later when it was found in a hole in the beam of a parish garret.

During the Directoire period, the Regent and other diamonds were pawned to a Berlin banker for four million francs to keep fourteen French armies in the field. It was redeemed and used as a guarantee for a loan from a Dutchman. Then it was recovered once again. Napoleon Bonaparte had it set in the hilt of a sword he carried when he was proclaimed Emperor of France.

In 1887, the French crown jewels were sold at auction, but the Regent was reserved and put on exhibition at the Louvre, among certain French treasures. But when the Germans invaded Paris in 1940, it was taken to the chateau country, where it was hidden behind a stone panel. After World War II, it was returned to the Louvre.

The Hope Diamond, now on display at the Smithsonian Institution, Washington, D.C., has become one of the best-known of the world's most famous diamonds. It is a forty-four-and-a-half-carat dark blue gemstone and was given its name by the man who purchased it in London in 1830—Henry Philip Hope. The stone has been surrounded by tragedy and, at one time, was believed to have been part of the original Blue Tavernier, brought from the Kollur mine in India to Europe by Jean Baptiste Tavernier, a French jeweler and traveler, famed for his handling of famous Indian diamonds. Tavernier bought the original stone in 1642 and from it the Hope diamond was cut. It was the largest of the three gems that were cut from the Blue Tavenier. The stone remained in the Hope family from 1830 until 1908, when it was sold, supposedly in partial liquidation of Lord Hope's debts. It passed to Abdul Hamid II, Sultan of Turkey, then to Pierre Cartier, a Paris jeweler.

In 1911 it was sold to Edward B. McLean, owner of the *Washington Post* newspaper, as a gift for his wife. After acquiring the gem, Mrs. McLean lost her child in an accident, saw her family break up, and committed suicide after losing her fortune. After her death in 1947, Harry Winston, a New York City gem merchant, purchased the stone and presented it to the Smithsonian in 1958.

Other famous diamonds include the historic Cullinan, discovered in the Premier mine in South Africa in 1905. It weighed 3,106 carats (more than a pound) prior to cutting, and may have been a cleavage fragment from a considerably larger stone. When the Cullinan was cut, it produced a total of 105 gems. From it came the Star of Africa, 530.2 carats of shimmering beauty—the largest cut diamond in existence. The Cullinan was the largest gem-quality diamond crystal ever found.

The history of refining, or processing diamonds also deserves consideration. This has been a gradual process over the centuries; now it involves bringing rough crystals from the mines and, through modern technology, creating the gems so highly prized by millions throughout the world. This involves the process of cutting, shaping, and polishing —a process which has brought the diamond from little more than a very durable substance used for medicinal purposes, into the realm of industry and jewelry. The actual contemporary methods used to process diamonds will be considered in a later chapter. Here we will discuss the process in terms of its evolution, or its development in history.

Superstition surrounding the stone in Europe probably delayed the development of diamond processing until the fourteenth century. The same holds true for India, since superstition also played its role there in the history of diamonds. At the core of the superstition was the following belief: to alter a diamond meant to destroy its magical powers.

Actually, poor documentation makes this part of the history of diamonds a mystery. The earliest known writings on the subject refer only to polishing. This indicates that the actual faceting of diamonds, or the planing of surfaces to bring about a particular shape, was confined to a cutting process only. It is possible that octahedral crystals were either left in their natural condition or altered by cutting, since they were called "point-cut stones."

Tavernier, in the seventeenth century, noted that considerable differences existed between cutting techniques in Europe and India. He reasoned that facets were used in India to hide flaws.

The shape of contemporary diamonds as gems is a result of the natural shape of the rough crystal—the octahedron, or double-pyramid (eight-sided stones with points at either end). Early techniques (in about the fifteenth century) probably involved grinding or polishing off one of the points to produce a square, table-cut diamond. Two hundred years later, more facets were added and the shape of the diamond was becoming more rounded. The procedure continued to develop until 1919. A book of theory was written at this time, in which the angles were documented and shown to produce a maximum amount of light and fiery color through multifacets. This brought about the fifty-eight facets of the modern gem diamond, cut in such a way that more light is reflected back into the viewer's eyes. A reduction in light leakage through the back is brought about through accurate cutting and polishing.

In the earliest days of diamond-cutting, other diamonds were used to accomplish the task, since only another diamond can be used in the process. When diamonds were used only as talismans, there was little or no incentive to polish and shape them. A fourteenth-century work from India, the *Agastimata*, told of a diamond finishing process using other diamonds, but included a warning that polishing a diamond on a wheel would result in the loss of magical powers.

CHAPTER 3

The Nature of Diamonds

DIAMOND—A WORD WHICH awakens beauty, mystery, and romance, a gem revered for centuries and credited as both poison and miracle drug—is a natural paradox. It is at once the hardest substance known to man, yet it will shatter into bits and pieces if struck at the proper point.

Chemically, it is pure carbon (the same material that makes up soot or graphite in a lead pencil). There are important differences, however. Definite natural requirements must be present for diamond to form far below the surface of the earth. Among those requirements are terrific heat and pressure. The carbon—specifically crystalline carbon—must first be trapped in molten lava; in fact, the lava itself must be of a specific chemical composition. As the crystals of carbon are trapped in this way, they are forced into a degree of compact hardness not known in any other substance. The uniqueness of diamond is that the formations are of definite patterns, a type of alignment which adds strength to the stone's structure and, at the same time, provides that certain brittleness which makes diamond susceptible to breakage.

Consequently, when a diamond is struck with a sufficiently strong blow from the critical angle, the gem shatters along the alignments of the structure, actually disintegrating. However, in other instances, a diamond can be utilized as an otherwise indestructible substance.

Because of the stringent conditions under which diamonds are formed, they are a rare substance. Instead of undergoing the necessary steps to form diamond, nature allows carbon to appear in other, more commonplace forms. Actually, carbon is the most common element in nature. Even the human body is one-eighth carbon, while the carbon content of wood is 50 percent. It is present in almost everything.

Diamond displays a hardness incomparable to any other substance known. The next hardest substance is corundum. Diamond is eight-five times harder than corundum. In fact, when an industrial diamond is properly set in a tool to be used for grinding and shaping, it can be used on a lathe to wear away two large emery (another form of corundum) wheels—one and a half feet in diameter and an inch thick—before the diamond shows any wear, even to the trained eye.

The specific gravity, or heaviness, of a cubic inch of diamond is three and a half times that of a cubic inch of pure water. Although this is not spectacular when compared to the specific gravity of iron, for example, it is an interesting fact since other forms of carbon have a specific gravity of only one and a half times that of water.

When measuring diamonds, the term "carat" is used. This is a measure of weight and it is a determining factor in assessing value. One metric carat is 1/2,268 of a pound, or 1/142 of an ounce, or 1/5 of a gram.

Another important consideration in the value (and certainly the beauty) of a diamond is its color. Why diamonds appear as one color rather than another we do not know for certain. On occasion, diamonds have been discovered which have pronounced color. These are called "fancies" and may be canary yellow, golden brown, blue, green, pink, violet, or even red. But fancy diamonds are rare. It is estimated that out of a hundred carats coming from mining operations, none will be fancy. The percentage of diamonds that will have defects in the crystal structure—which make them not as desirable for jewelry as gem-quality diamonds—depends on the source of the mine from which they are taken. This quality of diamond is called "bort." About 22 percent will probably be well crystallized but possess poor color, or color in varying degrees of yellow, brown, gray, or black.

Of the originally mined carats, less than one-fourth can be classified for sale as gems. These will possess varying degrees of color, most of them in only slight traces. However, when the diamond is subjected to light, this color is displayed through refraction. This produces the stone's flash, or fire. Refraction is simply light which bends as it passes from the air through a particular substance. By putting a stick into water, the stick appears bent; this, too, is refraction. Actually, it is an illusion caused by refraction of light. The same is true of a diamond, but to a far greater degree. The diamond has the highest index of all gemstones in its ability to refract light.

The diamond's ability to refract light to such a great degree is a result of its power to gather the light coming from all directions, then bending it into the center of the stone.

It is impossible to see through a well-cut diamond. As a result of the varying surfaces on a cut diamond, light is

Great Chrysanthemum

Oppenheimer

Hope

Regent

Hortensia

HISTORICAL GEMS OF THE WORLD
All color pictures courtesy N. W. Ayer & Son, Inc., except where otherwise indicated.

Earth Star

Arkansas

Niarchos

Cullinan*

Idol's Eye

Eugenie Blue

Kimberly

Koh-i-noor*

Jubilee

iffany

36c

Transvaal Blue

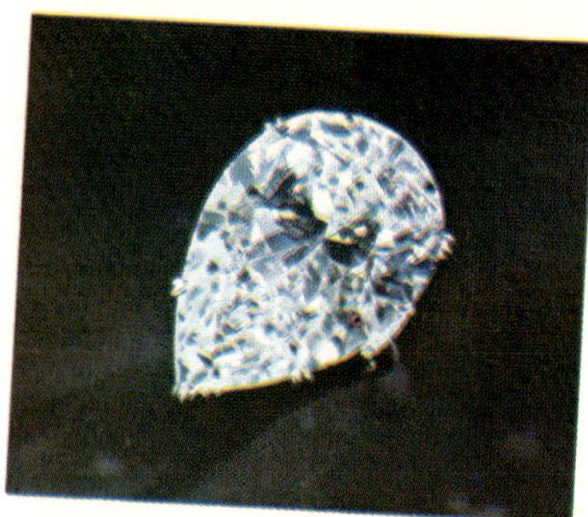

Taylor-Burton

Briolette of India

Black Orloff

Sultan of Morocco

refracted in a myriad of directions, bouncing back and forth, creating brilliance and fire.

Because of this ability to refract light, a diamond possesses a high degree of brilliance when properly cut for gemstone use. And proper cutting makes best use of the sharp, critical angles possible within the properties of the stone, properties which are exposed through proper cutting and polishing procedures.

In addition to its refractive capabilities, diamond also disperses light, or separates "white" light into its basic colors: red, orange, yellow, green, blue, and violet. This occurs when a ray of white light enters a dense substance—and a diamond is a very dense substance, the light is then refracted according to each color. And each color is refracted to a different extent, varying from red, which is bent the least, to violet, which is bent the most. Of all precious stones, diamond separates colors to the widest degree. As a result, when you rotate a diamond under light, slowly and gradually, fiery sports of color flash from the surfaces, each separate from the other.

Diamond is thought to melt around 3700 degrees Centigrade. But it will change color at much lower degrees of heat. Heat treatment at 500-900 degrees C for several hours turns most green irradiated diamonds to yellow or cinnamon brown, which is often considered a more attractive color than the green. Although it is legal to alter the color of a diamond artificially, this fact must be transmitted during any sales agreement.

These are some of the physical properties of diamond. But there are other characteristics of this "gem among gems" which make it unique among all the gemstones of the world.

All diamonds possess the physical properties outlined above. However, the quality of a diamond depends on other factors; these involve the best strategic use of the diamond's physical properties for jewelry and industrial use.

It is the quality of a diamond which determines its beauty and durability. Quality is revealed in variations of color gradations, imperfections in the structure of the stone, and proportions of the diamond which contribute to its ability to disperse light; the finish of the cut diamond determines its reflective qualities through the finished proportions.

There is no difference in the arrangement of the carbon atoms in diamonds. But differences in crystallization can produce imperfections which may appear as internal fractures; these are known in the diamond industry as "feathers" or "cloudy texture." During the process of formation, diamond (the mineral) undergoes many changes, some of which involve the presence of other minerals within the diamond itself. These fragments of other minerals appear in the stone as inclusions. There is the possibility that crystals of smaller diamonds may become enveloped within a larger diamond; these can be observed under certain light conditions as colorless "bubbles" or black "carbon spots." They are recognized as flaws or imperfections in the stone and contribute to the grading of the diamond for the gem market. These are all flaws in crystallization.

In addition, diamonds experience flaws in the finishing process. "Nicks" or fractures on the girdle, or rim of the stone, which occur in wearing or remounting, are considered finishing blemishes. Occasionally, "naturals," or tiny particles of the skin of the rough diamonds, are left on the girdle by the diamond cutter. Some dealers do not consider naturals as imperfections of finish. There also are shallow surface scratches which may be polished out with ease.

There are, then, two general types of blemishes which affect the quality of a diamond: internal and external flaws.

The former are caused in the natural formation process of the stone, and the latter are caused by the finishing process.

Eight types of internal blemishes will be considered briefly as they pertain to diamond quality:

1. Solid inclusion; this may be black or white and vary from a pinpoint to a large mass.
2. Bubble; this is transparent and round in appearance and can either be very small or fairly large in size.
3. Cloud; as implied by the name, this is a group of very tiny transparent bubbles or inclusions too small to be seen individually, but which combine to give the diamond a cloudy appearance.
4. Feathers (or glets, the Dutch name); when viewed from a flat-on perspective, this is usually a cleavage crack (following the grain of the crystal) which looks like a feather.
5. Butterfly; an inclusion with cleavage crack surrounding it which appears like the wings of a butterfly when viewed from certain directions.
6. Crack; a fracture which appears in a different direction than that of a cleavage (not according to the grain).
7. Knot (or naat, the Dutch name); this usually is a minor feature and occurs rarely. It appears as a twinning, usually visible externally, and also internally, if the twinned area is a different color from the remainder of the stone.
8. Fezels; these appear as shallow, white, wispy inclusions in a twinning plane.

There are nine external features, most of which are self-explanatory by the names given them; these all affect the quality of a diamond:

1. Scratches;
2. Chips and nicks;
3. Pits or cavities;

4. Flats on the girdle;
5. Naats on the surface;
6. Polishing lines;
7. Burn marks caused during the polishing process;
8. Naturals near the girdle;
9. Bearded girdle (the appearance of fuzziness around the rim of the diamond when viewed from above the flat surface).

It is quite easy to see that there is no such thing as a perfect diamond, if that term is used in an "ultimate" sense. *All* diamonds will reveal certain characteristics which can be interpreted as detracting from perfection.

A more proper term, and one that is acceptable to diamond experts, merchants, and customers alike, is "flawless." This simply means there are no internal or external blemishes visible on the diamond when it is examined under certain conditions—for example, a 10-power (10X) loupe under ideal lighting conditions. This is not to say that the diamond is perfect, for if it were to undergo extensive laboratory examination, it might reveal certain characteristics which could be construed as contributing to its imperfection.

Additionally, the term "perfect" is ambiguous. "Perfect" to one diamond retailer may mean no visible surface or interior blemishes, while others may use the term in reference to diamonds which have no surface blemishes.

CHAPTER 4

The Location and Mining
of Diamonds

EARLY DIAMOND DISCOVERIES occurred in the beds of both active and inactive rivers, or in the alluvial gravels in the banks. This type of location probably caused the Alexandrian astronomer Ptolemy (A.D. 90-168) to write of a diamond river somewhere in India.

Alluvial diamond finds occurred in India as early as 800 B.C. They were discovered in compact sandstones and conglomerates and in the sands and gravels of riverbeds and terraces.

At the beginning of the eighteenth century, Brazil became the location for new discoveries of diamonds. Gold miners, working in the gravels of riverbeds near Tujuco in Minas Geraes near the eastern coast of Brazil, discovered diamond crystals. One story tells of gold miners who apparently used the crystals for counters in card games until an official, Bernardo da Fonseca Lobo, who had seen diamond crystals in India, recognized them. Some were sent to Lisbon, others were cut in Amsterdam. The result was the discovery of diamonds in Brazil that were equal in quality to those found in India.

In 1725, records show that the Portuguese officially discovered diamonds in Brazil, then occupied the country. As more and more deposits were discovered, production increased until the market was nearly saturated. Prices dropped drastically and the Portuguese government was forced to severely restrict production. Mining was made a Portuguese royal monopoly in 1772.

Then, in 1844, another large diamond find occurred at Bahia, almost midway to the north, up the coast from Minas Geraes. In 1882 Brazil had gained its independence, but control was lacking to such a degree the deposits were worked too intensively. Within two decades the mines were virtually exhausted. The tough, black, impure diamond was found in the Chapida Diamantina area of Bahia, often in large lumps of several ounces. It became known as carbonado and it was of no commercial value at the time. Later it was discovered to have considerable value as an industrial abrasive.

All the Brazilian diggings were made in alluvial areas or in sandy soil deposited by flowing rivers.

Today, India and Brazil are famous in history only as deposits for diamonds. Despite the fact that India reigned supreme as the diamond nation of the world for 1,200 years, both Brazil and India have been worked too extensively in diamond mining to be considered strategic areas now.

Instead, the major emphasis has shifted to Africa, where the diamond finds have eclipsed all other areas, producing a massive 320 million carats from about 1890 to 1960 in South and South West Africa alone. The current annual production is running at around 8 million carats.

Diamonds first were discovered in Africa near the community of Hope Town on the banks of the Orange River in South Africa. A story that equals the card-playing Brazilian gold miners surrounds the African find.

A poverty-stricken family by the name of Jacobs lived in a hut near Hope Town on the DeKalk farm. In 1866, as the children of the family played outside one day, they picked up a bright pebble during one of their games. They brought it home and dropped it on the floor of the farmhouse. A neighbor, Schalk van Niekerk, asked Vrouw Jacobs the next day if she would sell the stone. She laughed and gave it to him. Van Niekerk gave it to a trader, John O'Reilly, and asked him to find out if it had any value. O'Reilly showed it to several friends on his way up the Orange River, but no one was able to identify the one-time plaything.

Van Niekerk had been given a book on precious stones by a land surveyor who had seen van Niekerk's collection (colorful stones and pebbles he had picked up from the river and the veldt). The book noted that diamond would scratch glass. So van Niekerk took the "pebble" and scratched a windowpane with it. A deep mark was made. The windowpane still exists and is now on display in the Colesberg Museum.

After being unable to determine the identity of the mysterious stone, O'Reilly sent it to Dr. W. G. Atherstone of Grahamstown, a noted geologist, who identified it as a twenty-one-carat diamond worth $2,500.

It was ten months before another diamond was discovered, despite the almost frantic efforts of both Boers and their black servants, following the find by the Jacobs' children. The second discovery was thirty miles downstream from Hope Town, near the junction of the Orange and Vaal rivers.

Another two years passed. In March of 1869, an eighty-three-and-a-half carat stone was picked up by a witch doctor on the banks of the Orange. Again, van Niekerk, who happened to be a stepson of Jacobs', bought the stone. This time he paid for it with five hundred sheep, ten oxen, and a horse. However, he sold it for $55,000 and it became known as the famed "Star of South Africa."

The Star of South Africa really started the rush of diamond hunters to that country. As they came, they concentrated their efforts along the Vaal River near the town of Barkly West where many flawless diamonds had been dug from the sands. These were adventurers from all walks of life: gold miners from Canada and Australia, Europeans, deserting seamen, honest men, and rabble—all poured into South Africa on every ship docking there. But the trip from ship to diamond field was even more grueling than any sailing at sea. There was a lengthy trek across the veldt, over the desert of the Karoo, and over the mountains to the scorched, rocky land. Some two to four months later, after averaging ten miles a day, they reached the south banks of the Orange in the north portion of Cape Colony. Some went across the Orange into what was known as the Orange Free State, while others traveled north to the Vaal and into the land of the Griquas.

Most of them knew nothing of diamond mining. A few of them had worked diamond mines in India, Borneo, or Brazil. For the most part, they were an untried bunch at diamond mining. And they came by the thousands. Difficulties were immediate, including dissension with the neighboring Boer farmers whose sheep kept falling into the diggings and breaking legs, or just ending up in a digger's supperpot over a fire.

The claims they worked were small—thirty-one feet square. But the claims could be worked extremely deep—up to two hundred feet—with the dirt being washed for the occasional stones it yielded.

In 1871, a shantytown known as Kimberley, sprang up in an area near, but not adjacent to, the Riet, Modder, Vaal, and Hartz Rivers. Ten thousand miners worked, sweated, fought, and dug their way into the earth. Today Kimberley ranks as the greatest of all diamond mining areas.

By 1889, the pit at Kimberley was a cavernous abyss, one-quarter of a mile across at the rim and 1,300 feet deep. Rock slides at the bottom already had taken scores of lives, and working in this area had become almost suicidal. Kimberley was great not only because of the finds that were made there, but because of the ease in working the area. At top ground was the yellow dirt in great circular deposits; this could be worked as deeply as one cared to go. But it was found that the yellow ground graded into a hard rock and took on a greenish blue color, still bearing diamonds. Crisscrossing the honey-combed likeness of the area, were systems of ropes with buckets attached which served as hauling operations to bring the ore to the top. It was kept in operation by horse-drawn windlasses or steam engines. It was like an inset kingdom with the gouged-out earth, the criss-crossing web-like rope systems, and the men working in a fever. The whole scene was not unlike that of an ant hill.

The fertile blue ground was found to lie within a five-hundred-foot circle at the bottom of the mine, and it still contained diamonds. It appeared to be inexhaustible.

Geologists concluded that the deposit at the base of the mine was the root of an ancient volcano—a mountain stripped away eons earlier through the passage of even more eons of time. The blue rock beneath, which became known as the diamond "pipe," was all that remained of the volcano.

Proper study of the Kimberley mine must include the

methods used to extricate diamonds from the pipe. The open-type mining that had taken so many lives by 1889 and was constantly endangering thousands more, had to be abandoned. The owners of the Kimberley pit sank a shaft a thousand feet from the rim of the open mine where the rock was solid and cave-ins were not a threat. A blasting operation began. It took months and even years to do it, but a depth of 2,500 feet was eventually reached. At intervals, tunnels would be bored off the main shaft, below the bottom of the nearby pit. Thousands of tons of blue earth were sent to the surface by this method.

The fantastic proportions of available diamonds in this area is illustrated by drawing circles on a map, using Kimberley as the center. By drawing the circles at ten-mile intervals, a distance of a hundred and twenty miles, some one hundred claims had been located in that area by 1890. However, it was the pipe mine at Kimberley which became the most productive.

Similar stories unfold around all other pipe mines in South Africa—and there are more than two hundred known pipe mines; most of them, however, are not profitable enough to work anymore. De Beers, Jagersfontein, and Dutoitspan are gaping holes with miles of dark, murky tunnels beneath the surface. The Wesselton and the great Premier mine near Pretoria have combined with the other five South African mines to give the world considerably more than a hundred million carats of glistening diamonds.

The Republic of Zaire, which was formerly the Belgian Congo, has become another source of diamonds in recent decades. As early as 1906 it was known that the infested jungles of this undeveloped land contained diamonds. But the only access to the area at the time was by means of steam launches traveling up the Congo River and its branch tributary, the Kasai. All supplies had to be brought in by steam launch. It wasn't until 1910 that a discovery in the gravels of the Diminina River near the Mai Muene waterfall began the history of the Congo mines.

By the time the field was identified, it stretched 150,000 square miles and included many ancient river beds; it extended into neighboring Angola, which was held by the Portuguese. It was the world's largest source of diamonds.

A group of American geologists led the party which discovered the field, and it was placed under the operation of a Belgian Company, the "Societe Internationale Forestiere et Miniere du Congo."

Although it is the largest field known to the world, most of the diamonds which are extracted from it are suitable for industrial use only. They are mostly brown or gray bort. Gem diamonds are found to a greater degree in the Angola portion of the field.

Since the Congo has become a republic, Forminiere, the shortened version for the name of the operating company, has been worked by the government with the assistance of technical advisors from the diamond mining industry. The Angola portion of the field has been worked by a company known as Diamang, the Companhia de Diamantes de Angola.

The center of the Congo workings is the community of Tshikapa in the Kasai region. About fifty large pits exist from which the diamond crystal-bearing gravel is taken.

There are other African mines as well; the Gold Coast Colony, now Ghana, in West Africa, is one area where a field was discovered. Geologists also have found deposits further west along the coast, in Sierra Leone, where the diamond crystals yield a higher-than-average gem content, mostly gemstones.

Other nations also produce some diamond fields. Among them are Guyana (formerly British Guiana), Venezuela,

Borneo, Indonesia, Australia, Russia, and isolated small finds in the United States.

An interesting note about the Russian finds is that diamonds occasionally were found in placer deposits in the Ural Mountains of Russia by gold miners. However, when the region was geologically explored, it was evident that there were no pipes. Later, the vast area between the Uenisei and Lena Rivers in Siberia was explored, following a geological determination that a platform zone was in existence similar to that of Africa and India where diamonds had been found. A large expedition was formed in 1947 to explore the central and eastern Siberia regions. One year later, in the upper areas of the Nizhnaya Tunguska River, the first diamonds were found. Alluvial deposits were found in several areas, including the bed of the Vilyui River, but no pipes were located.

At last in 1953, persistence paid off, after the discovery of Pyrope garnets; this indicated the presence of diamonds. A concentration of more prospecting in the same neighborhood led to the discovery of the first kimberlite pipe in the upper Markha River region.

From 1954 on, another four hundred or so pipes and seams were located, but only about one in forty proved to hold diamonds. The richest find is the Mir (Peace) pipe in the basin of the Lesser Batoubiya tribuary to the Vilyui.

There are massive mining problems in digging out the diamonds Russia has to offer, especially in the Siberian area, since the soil is permanently frozen and only the top few yards of ground thaw in the summer. The permafrost affects alluvial as well as pipe deposits, since the gravels are cemented in ice even in the summertime.

In the United States, a diamond mine exists in the southwestern part of Arkansas. It was discovered in 1906. Geologists examined the rocks and found a pipe of blue ground quite similar to the one in South Africa. The largest crystal recovered weighed forty carats, but usually it takes three to four Arkansas stones to make a carat. The mine has been idle for several years now, with little or no activity taking place. It is now a diamond park where, for a fee, you may dig your own diamonds.

To discuss the location of diamonds only in respect to the nations where they are found surely presents an incomplete picture, for there is a geology about diamonds which determines their location. As explained above, diamond is found in the alluvial soils and gravels of riverbeds as well as in the rock in which it is formed. South Africa is one of the few places in the world where diamond is found within formative rock. Therefore, South Africa is the key to the geology of diamonds. This blue ground of South Africa consists of basic igneous rock; that is, it contains no quartz whatsoever, and was formed from cooling lava. Quartz is among the most common of earth's materials; the grains of sand on the beach are made of quartz. From geological studies, it appears that blue ground is a basic condition of diamond formation. Blue ground gets its name from a process which occurred when the mass of igneous rock was cooling. Olivine, a glassy, grass-green mineral peculiar to this type of rock, was then attacked by chemical solutions and most of it became serpentine—a dark, greenish-blue, rather soft mineral which gives the ground its color and name.

Deep beneath the surface of the earth, which now reflects its blue ground contents, seething gasses and fiery masses of molten mineral began to develop immense pressure on the carbon deposits millions of years ago. As the pressure began to build, these gasses began to work on the heated masses of material which slowly started to seep through cracks and fissures, until they cracked through the earth's crust in a tremendous explosion, boring a clean, round hole at the surface. Molten rock began to well up in the hole and spread over the surface of the land, bringing with it the diamonds formed far below. Layers of this molten rock built up to form a mountainous volcano. When the pressure at last was relieved, the mountain cooled and hardened; deep beneath the surface, carbon deposits of diamond were formed. Millions of years passed and streams and rivers formed, slowly eating into the dormant volcano. Diamonds from the upper layers went downstream, to be discovered in the sands by prospectors.

A point should be made here concerning the existence of diamond crystals within this rock. For every ton of blue ground mined, less than one-eighth of a carat of crystal is recovered. This means that only *one part of rock in thirty-five million, by weight, is diamond*. Of that part, three-fourths of it is worthless for jewelry. And this ratio exists only in the richest of mines such as those in South Africa. It is easy to imagine the millions of tons of earth which must be mined to produce gems from the less lucrative mines.

Additionally, I would like to mention the existence of diamonds in river diggings. Throughout the face of the earth flowing water has formed rivers, streams, creeks, and brooks, lifting and taking with it solid rock, and loose debris of mud and sand. The more swift the river, the larger the size of the rock that is carried along with the flow of the water. The slower the stream, the finer the sediment which is deposited along the way.

The Orange River in South Africa is an intermittent river, slowing to a trickle during long dry spells, but becoming a torrent of raging water during heavy summer thunderstorms. The Vaal and smaller streams which feed the Orange act in the same manner throughout the year. Therefore, all of these bodies of water have worked together to bring diamond-bearing crystals far from their origin beneath the earth.

The possibility of finding a massive stone that will make life a financial breeze from that point on, keeps compulsive gamblers like prospecting diamond diggers working river beds for years. A case in point was Jacobus Jonker, some sixty or so years old, who had worked the river beds his entire life for a pittance. Not an impatient man, Jonker continued his efforts until January, 1934, when, not far from the Premier Mine in South Africa, he discovered a 726-carat crystal that brought him more than $300,000 to enjoy in his later years.

CHAPTER 5

The Extraction (Mining) of Diamonds

Interspersed throughout the history of the diamond industry, there are a number of men who have lived their lives shaping this fascinating business. In so doing, many gave their names to several aspects of the extraction process— the process of bringing diamonds from the ground to the marketplace.

The names of some of these individuals will remain forever enshrined in the mining companies they helped found and develop. Others, who toiled in the fields, working to extract the elusive crystals and discover a fortune in the process, weren't out to become famous; in their operations, however, they perfected, or at least developed, methods which still bear their names. One of these was J. L. Babe, who went to South Africa in 1865 before the Vaal River diamonds were found. He did not represent mining interests as such, but was a representative of the Winchester Repeating Rifle Company. After five years in the field, Babe in-

Rough diamond. Deformed octahedral crystal, Kimberly, South Africa. (Reprinted by permission of Charles Scribner's Sons from *Color Under Ground* by Lee Boltin and John S. White, Jr. Photographs © 1971 Lee Boltin.)

ALLUVIAL DIAMOND MINING

Rotary washing pan,
South Africa.
(Courtesy Thomas Draper)

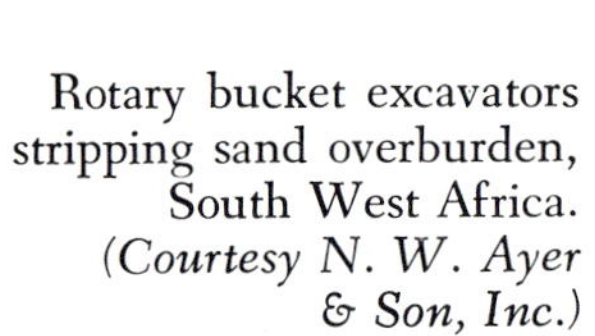

Rotary bucket excavators
stripping sand overburden,
South West Africa.
(Courtesy N. W. Ayer
& Son, Inc.)

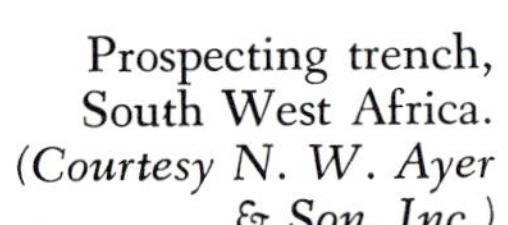

Prospecting trench,
South West Africa.
(Courtesy N. W. Ayer
& Son, Inc.)

Working alluvial deposit
by hand labor,
South West Africa.
(Courtesy N.W. Ayer
& Son, Inc.)

Stripping overburden
in stream bed after
diverting water.

Hydraulic mining.

Preparing to
dive for
diamond-bearing
gravels.

Screening and
checking concentrate.

DIAMOND MINING
(Courtesy N. W. Ayer & Son, Inc.)

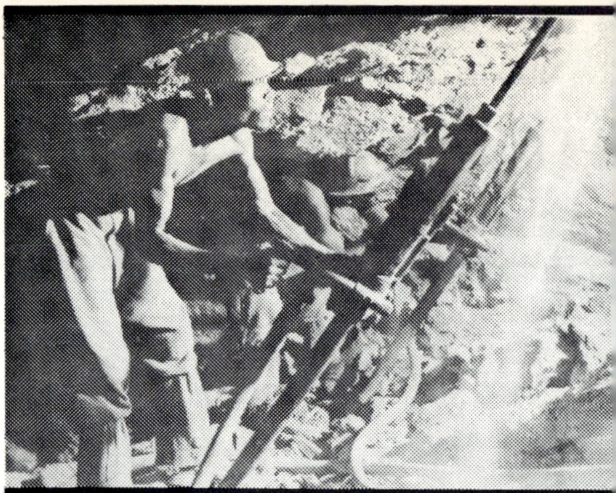

Drilling holes in blueground preparatory to blasting.

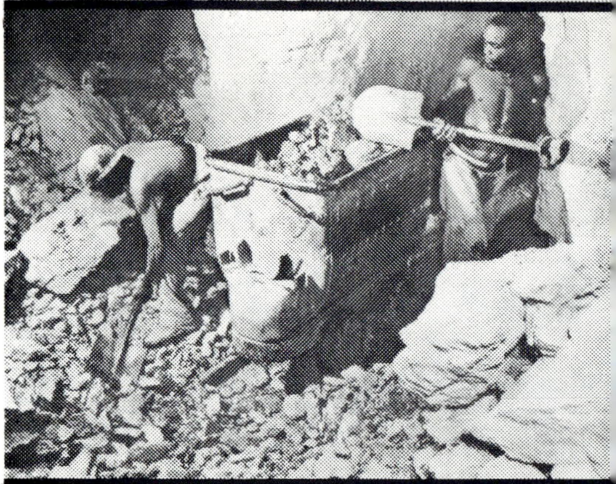

Loading blueground after blasting.

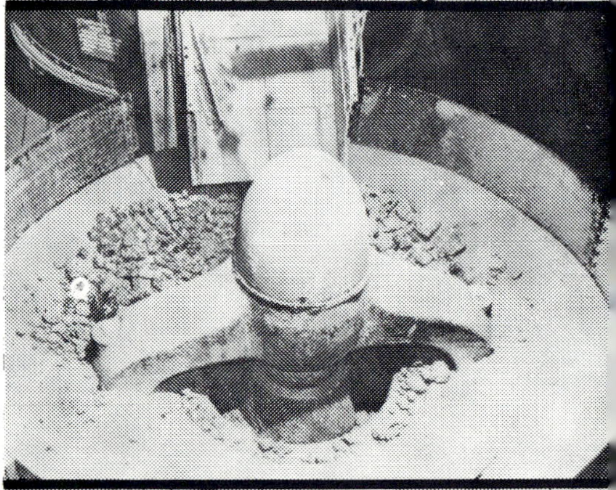

Crushing the blueground.

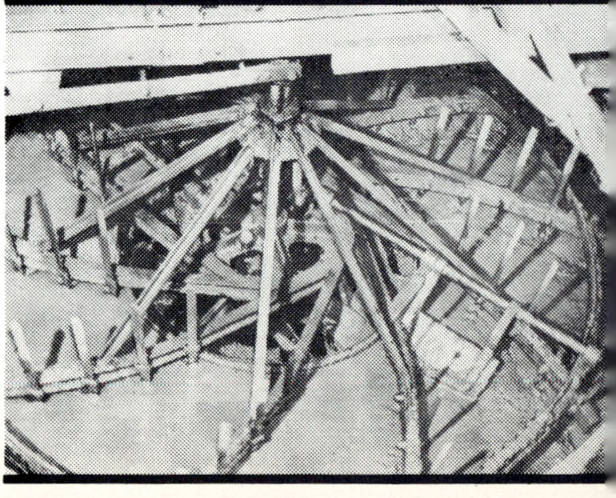

Rotary washing pan.

A tailings dump,
showing waste material
from the recovery plant.

Concentrates from
the washing process passing
over the grease table.

Diamonds adhering
to the grease table.

Sorting and classifying
the diamonds according
to size, shape, and quality.

Two views of the
Finsch Mine, South Africa.
(*Courtesy N. W. Ayer & Son, Inc.*)

Diamond mining via the chambering method.
(*Courtesy Gemological Institute of America*)

Grooving the
Vargas diamond
preparatory to cleaving it.

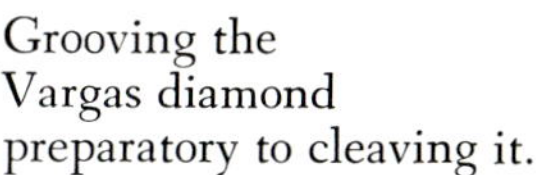

The Vargas diamond
marked for cleaving.

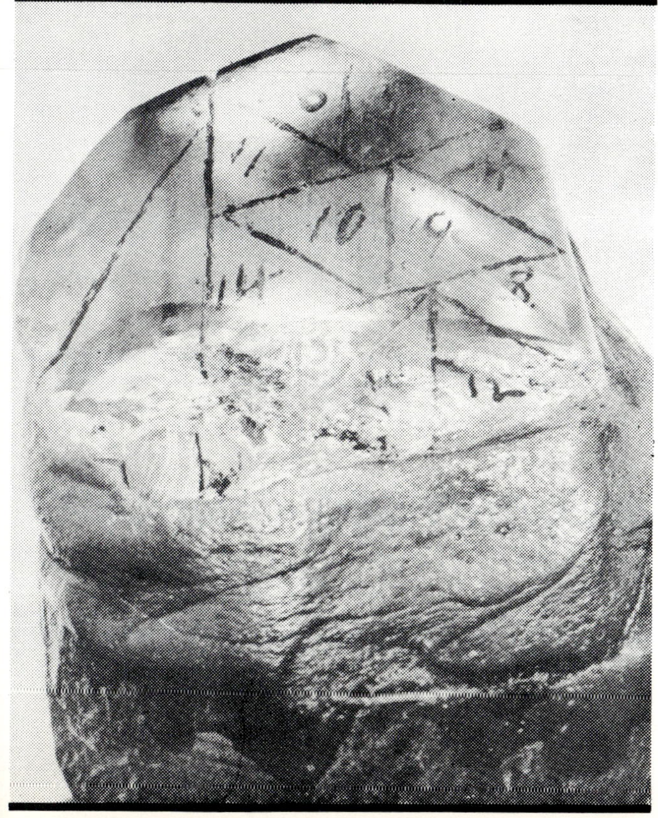

*(Courtesy N. W. Ayer
& Son, Inc.)*

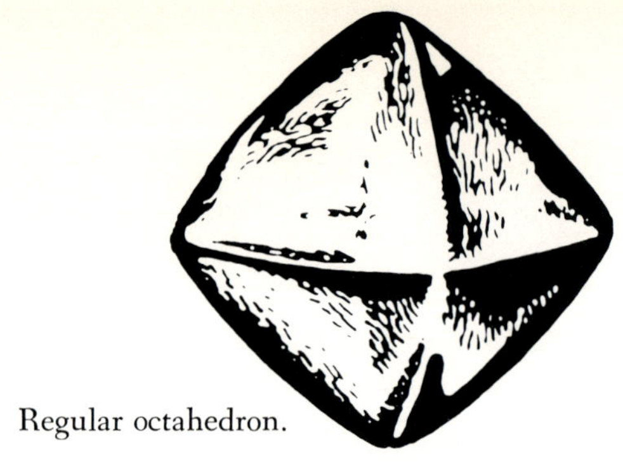

Regular octahedron.

DIAMOND CRYSTAL FORMATIONS

*(All courtesy
N. W. Ayer & Son, Inc.)*

Macle.

Irregular shape.

Flat.

Cleavage.

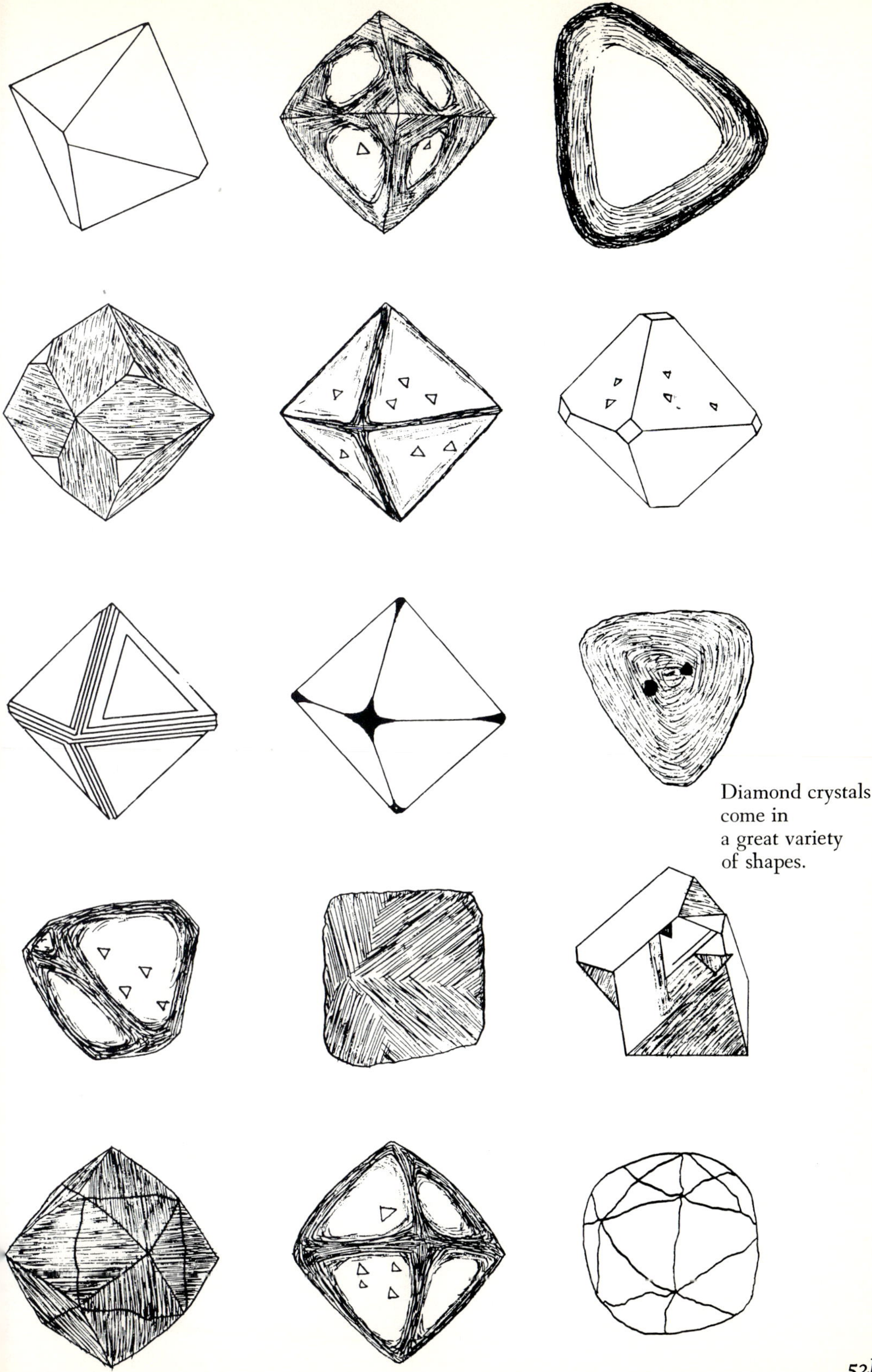

Diamond crystals
come in
a great variety
of shapes.

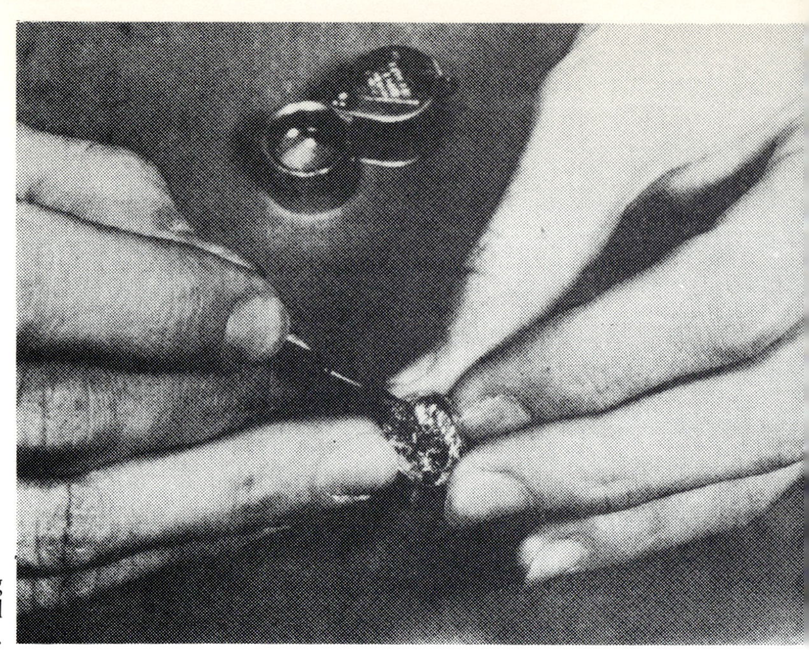

Marking
the diamond
for cutting.

DIAMOND CUTTING

(Courtesy N. W. Ayer & Son, Inc.

Diamond-sawing
machinery.

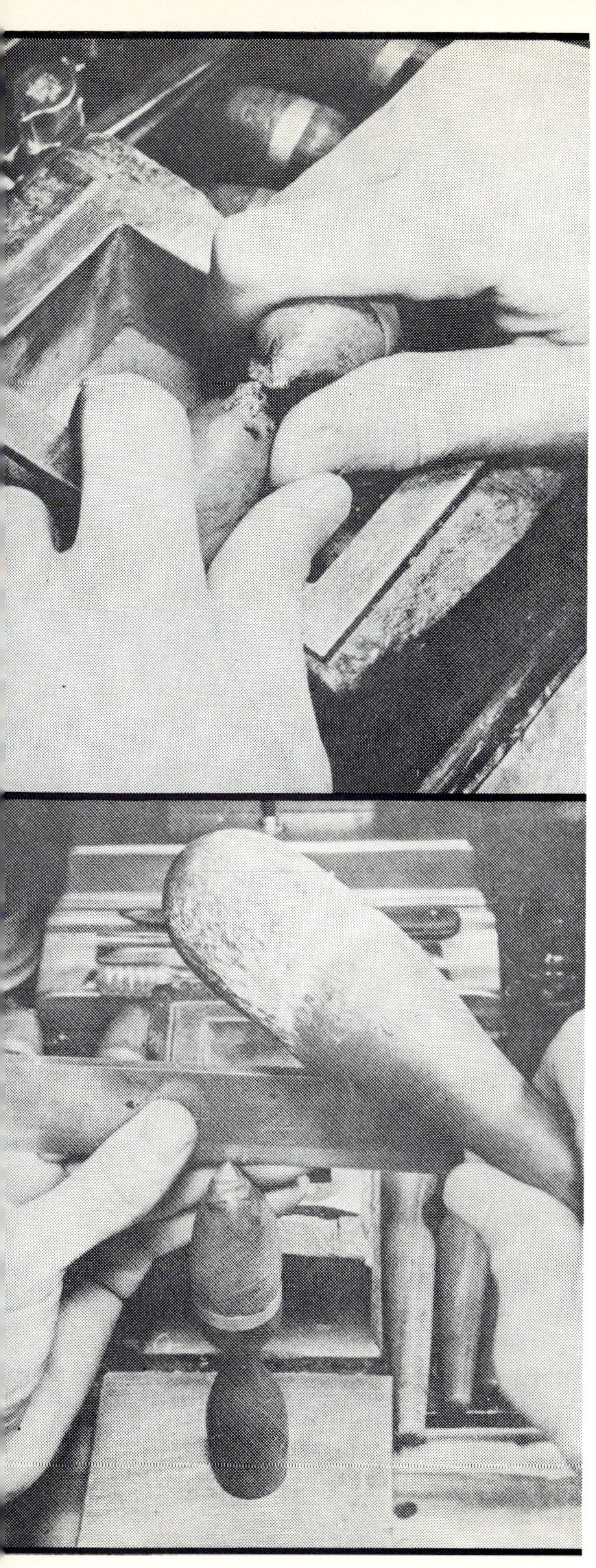

Cleaving the diamond.

DIAMOND CUTTING

Polishing the cut diamond.

(Courtesy N. W. Ayer & Son, Inc.)

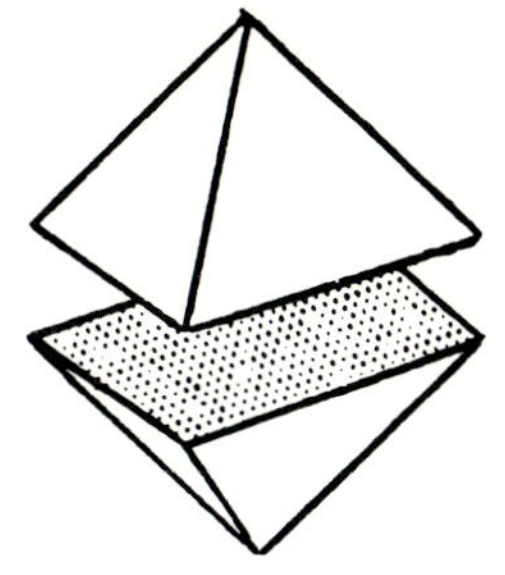
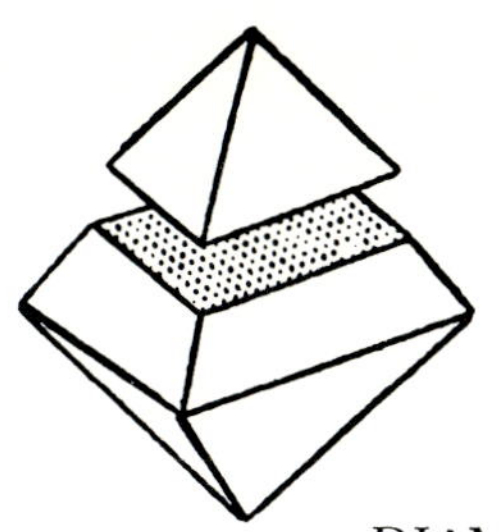

DIAMOND CUTTING

*(Courtesy Gemological
Institute of America)*

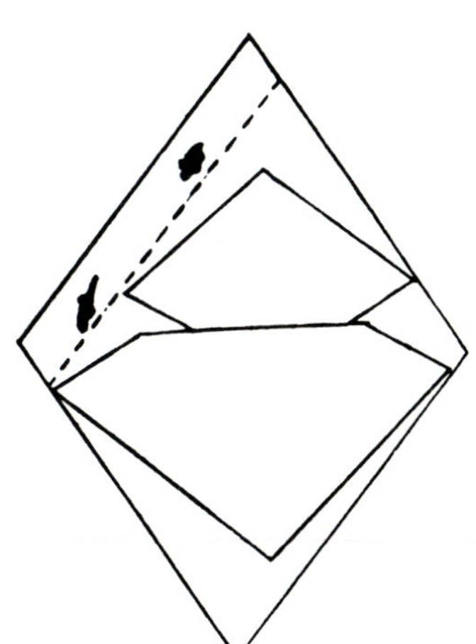
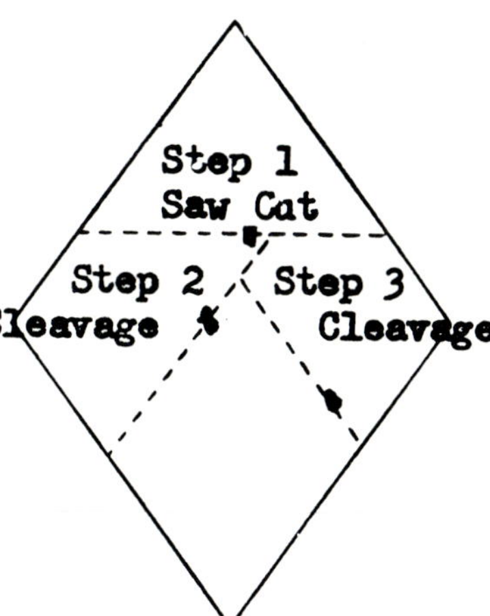

A diamond
diagrammed
for cutting.

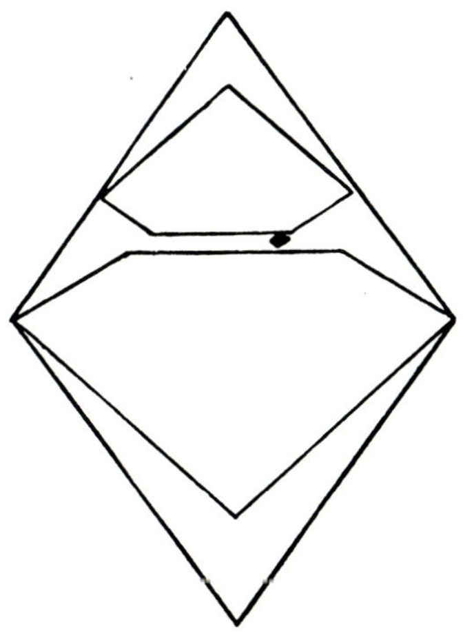

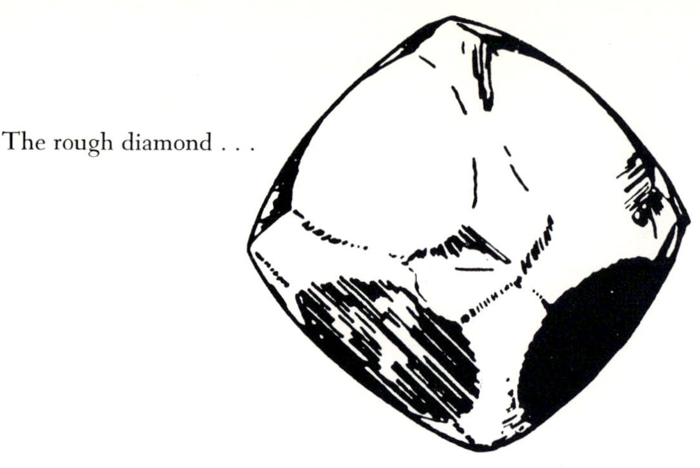

The rough diamond . . .

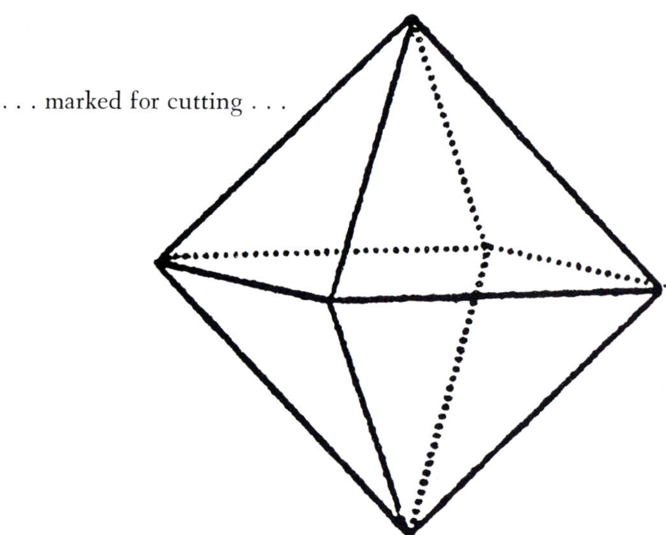

. . . marked for cutting . . .

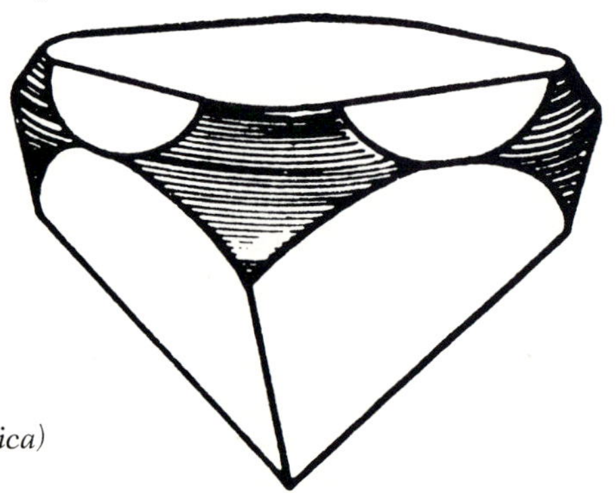

. . . has been sawed and partially faceted.

(Courtesy Gemological Institute of America)

52p

vented a rocking sieve which became known as the Baby, or Yankee Baby. Its importance to early diamond mining methods cannot be underestimated. Although it was not a complicated device, it aided recovery methods immeasurably.

The importance of the sieve is evident at the early river diggings where pits were gouged into the earth and the gravels extracted which contained the crystals. Miners using picks and shovels would dig out the gravels and, on dry days, immediately sift the material through a round sieve. The sieve had a large mesh and retained only stones about an inch in diameter. Few diamonds were found which would be retained in this initial sifting process, but if they were there, they could be located with ease.

Two other sifting processes were undertaken—one to remove the sand, and the other to recover the "middlings." Diamonds the size of grains of sand were not worth recovering, so the process to remove the sand left the middlings, which were taken to the river to be washed in a fine sieve, where whatever silt and dirt remained were removed. What was left—the middlings—were then searched for diamonds.

Babe was one of the few experienced miners who came to the South African fields in the 1860's. He had been a gold digger in California, and his background gave him the knowledge necessary to construct the simple sifting machine which would bear his name. He retired to the United States in 1873, having been so successful in using and selling his Yankee Baby that he accumulated sufficient wealth to afford the luxury of retirement.

The Baby was made of two sieves, one situated above the other. The main sieve was a large rectangular frame hung from four rawhide thongs, or light chains, from four posts planted in the ground. It was fed through a smaller sieve about two feet square with a mesh that allowed stones up to about a half inch in diameter to pass through. In one process, the larger material was discarded at one end, with the fine tailings remaining underneath. The middlings were deposited at the other end and were then taken to be washed and sorted.

Washing was an optional process; it could be undertaken before or after screening, depending on the amount of fine material contained in the deposit and on the availability and cost of water. Improvisation became necessary in constructing a form of cradle for use in washing. The simplest device consisted of a discarded gin box from England. This box was mounted on another gin box and rocked back and forth by the use of levers. It was used for dry sieving and for washing. When used for washing, water was poured from the top by a bucket. As time passed, more elaborate cradles were devised which were used both for sieving and washing.

These early principles of diamond mining have been retained; actually, changes have only been elaboration and refinements of the basic process. In the early days of mining, the variations of the basic methods depended on the area in which the mining took place. For example, at dry diggings, where the area was a semi-desert, the yellow ground was pulverized by sledge hammers and shoveled into rectangular hand sieves with holes one-eighth of an inch in diameter. There was no washing in these early years and the material that passed through the holes was thrown away and the remainder taken to picking tables where the crystals were removed.

This process was extremely unreliable, as a matter of fact, in recent years, mining companies have gone back and picked through the piles of tailings left by these early diggers. When reworked according to more efficient methods, these pilings have been found quite rich in crystals. In some areas, the old tailings have been reworked as much as three times through improved extraction methods.

Water became an important element in the mining process and the difficulty of obtaining water at dry, desert-like diggings made the mining processes there less efficient and reliable. In order to concentrate the heavier fractions of gravels, or to separate the materials of higher relative density from those of a lighter element, water is used. The term "concentrate" is used to define this heavier fraction of gravel.

Once the material taken from the earth has been screened and washed, it is emptied into a sieve about two feet, six inches in diameter, with a bottom of fine mesh. This sieve is held in a tub of water or in a river and sharply twisted back and forth, then moved up and down in a jiggling motion. The repetition of this process brings the lighter gravels to the top of the sieve with the heavier materials concentrated in the middle or the bottom of the sieve. Then the sieve is taken from the water to the picking table, where the contents are dumped into the form of a type of mud pie. The picker examines the stones on the top and middle of the pile, picking out any diamond crystals he may find. To make certain the "pie" contains no other diamond deposits, he slices through the mud gradually in order to extract whatever crystals it contains. A triangular piece of iron or aluminum about six inches long and three inches or less in width is used to cut off sections of the gravel and spread them across the sorting table.

This table used for picking and sorting the diamond crystals was simply a packing case at first. Then it was replaced by a rough table or trestle table covered with a sheet or iron. The covering sheet probably was either a flattened tin container nailed down or an enameled advertisement sheet.

As men continued to delve deeper into the earth, it became necessary to invent some sort of road system over which the miners could haul out their diggings and also exit and enter the mining area. At Kimberley it was decided that each claim would include a strip seven and a half feet wide which would not be worked, but would contribute to the roadway. The roadway system was a series of paths fifteen feet wide and forty-five feet apart. It was a practical solution initially, but as the claims went deeper and deeper, the sides of the roads began to crumble. Since the entire area around and including Kimberley was weathered yellow ground, it weathered further when exposed to the air, crumbling slowly as the pits went deeper.

The procedure used in the digs was to pick and shovel out the dirt, load it into sacks, and have laborers carry it up steps cut into the side of the claim. These sacks of dirt were then emptied at the side of the road. From there the material was taken to the edge of the mine and broken up, screened, and sorted.

It took only a few years for the roads to begin crumbling, forcing further innovations in the haulage system at Kimberley. By 1872 the roads were unsafe for use and by the mid-1870's they had disappeared altogether. To bring the deposits to the surface of the mine, aerial gear was devised.

At first the system consisted of a pulley fixed above and at the edge of the hole, with a second pulley below in the claim. A rope was wound around the pair of pulleys and a bucket, made of hide, was attached to this. A digger at the top wound the pulley in order to bring up the loaded bucket. By 1876 there were literally thousands of these pulley lines meshing across the gaping hole at Kimberley.

Further developments brought about iron or steel cables to replace the ropes, and large, steel, bucket-like bins replaced the hide containers. This evolved into a trolley system which ran on the cables. The trolley had a frame with four wheels and carried a container into which the yellow ground was placed. The wheels ran on two parallel cables and a separate rope attached to the trolley frame was used to draw the vehicle up the sloping cables. This rope was wound around a large drum, known as a "whim," and laborers would turn the whims to draw up the trolleys. Horses were sometimes used; later steam engines were introduced.

Down in the claim, hundreds of feet below the surface or ridge of the mine, a platform was used for filling the containers. At the top, the container automatically discharged its contents into a bin.

By 1875 another name had entered the history of diamond-mining techniques: J. Mackay. Mackay invented a hand-driven rotary washing pan which was simple in concept but even today its operating principle is not fully understood. In fact, the Diamond Research Laboratory in Johannesburg still has the system under study.

Mackay's invention was developed into an annular container which was four feet across and about nine inches deep. In the central hole was a vertical axle with four arms in the form of a cross, pivoted on top. Rows of knives extended downward from the arms of the cross and acted like rakes. The raw material from the digging was shoveled into the annular pan which had been filled with water. The rakes turned by winding a handle, and the result was a swilling motion of the water and gravel. The water overflowed the edge, with the lighter materials being held in suspension in the muddy water. Diamonds and the other heavier materials settled to the bottom. When the individual loads were separated in this fashion, the pan was emptied for picking.

The modern version of the rotary washing pan, still in use in the South African mines, is power-driven and considerably larger than the original system. A strange fact in the operation of the rotary pan (and the issue which is under study) is that lumps of kimberlite, with a specific gravity heavier than the muddy substance in which they are contained, float up and over when run through the rotary process.

So far, the descriptions of mining processes have centered around the yellow ground, or kimberlite, converted through the weathering of air and water. This material could be broken up easily and pulverized to release the crystals of diamond. But as the diggers went deeper into the earth, this material disappeared into unaltered kimberlite, or blue ground. At the Kimberley mine, blue ground was discovered about eighty feet below the surface.

Many miners thought they had found the limit of diamond-bearing earth when blue ground was reached. They sold their claims. Those who continued mining found that the blue ground was very difficult to break up. But they soon learned that lumps of the blue ground that were thrown aside, broke up after exposure to the air. About three months were needed before disintegration took place. Alternating weather was the most ideal condition for the disintegration of the blue ground exposed to air. When the weather was too dry, artificial watering aided the process. Also, gangs of laborers using the backs of shovels or mallets broke up the lumps.

Dangers continued to plague the mining operations. Near the surface of the pipes, the ground was so soft that the sides of the Kimberley mine were continually crumbling. The ground would crumble faster than it could be cleared away. By 1882, three tons of debris had to be removed before one ton of blue ground could be extracted.

At the De Beers mine, after miners had witnessed what was happening at Kimberley, an attempt was made to cut back the sides, but the methods available at that time did not work. At Dutoitspan, another South African mine, a rim of blue ground was retained as a protecting wall. The wall collapsed—fortunately when the mine was almost empty of workers.

In spite of the dangers, the blue ground was yielding diamonds, and methods had to be found to mine it as safely and profitably as possible. So the next step, which also came at Kimberley, was to sink a shaft. At first it was hoped the shaft could be drilled from the outside. But there was not enough money available for the operation, so it was decided to sink it from the inside, through the rubble on top of the blue ground. This method worked and several other shafts were sunk in other parts of the mine as well. Later, when Cecil Rhodes took control of Kimberley, sufficient financing was available to work a shaft from the outside of the pipe; by 1914, when operations ceased at that particular site, a depth of 3,601 feet had been reached.

Eventually, the blue ground became a honeycomb of chambers and stalls. The pillars, unable to support the shafts, began to crumble from the pressure of the rubble piled on top, and the mine had to be evacuated and a new point of entry found.

Next came a system which involved cutting chambers into the mine off the main shaft in a staggered manner so that the top of the blue ground formed a kind of hump beneath the overburden. The pressure from the overburden was relieved by a stair-step type of digging operation on the levels. The effect was to support the overburden at the sides like an arch. However, as a pipe is mined underground, the overburden of shale and rubble mixed with blue ground continues to build, descending in the pipe, causing more and more pressure. As various other systems were worked at the Kimberley, at even greater depths, this system became impractical.

Other methods evolved over the years in an ever-increasing effort to continue mining the available pipes until today a type of open-cast mining is used. It is systematic and thorough. Before the actual mining operation is begun, geologists sample the ground to determine the feasibility of even starting the procedure. All excavation is mechanized. The worked area is excavated in straight lines. Excavation of the yellow ground is accomplished in the middle of the mined area and proceeds in such a way that a spiral road winds out of the mine. Trucks haul out the deposit. Electric shovels and thirty-five-ton dump trucks operate on a twenty-four-hour basis. As the yellow ground is removed, the sides of the rock are cut back in steps to remove the risk of crumbling rubble that jeopardized the early mining operations. This procedure also increases the reliability of underground mining once it is undertaken. The result is a terraced, open pit. Modifications and developments exist in mines around the world, but this is the basic premise to open-cast mining.

The latest development in mining is undersea recovery of deposits. As early as 1900, diamonds were discovered on the coastal desert strip of South West Africa. The alluvial mining methods of Consolidated Diamond Mines of South West Africa Limited had revealed deposits on a narrow bedrock parallel to the coast. The diamonds found there are about ninety percent gem quality, and recovery is reputed to be almost one hundred percent efficient. It has been assumed that the diamonds came down the Orange River, since the distribution along the coast drops in a typical curve from the river mouth north up the coast. Supposedly, the diamonds in the beaches came down the Orange and were taken up the coast by the sea, some being trapped in potholes.

Diamonds have been recovered from the sea, but the cost of recovery is more than the crystals are worth. There is a prospecting ship called the *Rockeater*. This ship has been fitted with undersea drills which plot the payable areas of sea bed. The crystal-bearing gravels are fixed by radar and, another vessel, the *Pomona*, a recovery barge, is towed to the point where the gravels have been located. The *Pomona* is anchored in such a way that, as it moves forward, it also sweeps slowly across the area to be mined. Four vacuum tubes are fitted to the front of the barge—two large ones ahead, two smaller ones to pick up what is left by the main tubes. Water jets blow away the overburden of sand and silt, and through a special structure on the vacuum tubes, gravel is sucked up into the barge. A large amount of sea water is brought up into the barge, but this is removed and spewed back into the sea.

"Holding back" the sea in order to mine tidal areas is a formidable barrier to more extensive operations in ocean waters. Dams have been built and some success has been realized. But "tidal mining" remains more problem-ridden because dams must be built to last long enough to mine the area. A method has been found to hold back the water long enough in certain areas along the beach. It is the lower half of the beach, along the coast of South West Africa, where separate mining operations must be evolved and where the problems are far more complex.*

------

*As this book was going to press, it was learned that sea mining is being discontinued.

CHAPTER 6

The Extracting and Finishing of Diamonds

EXTRACTING DIAMONDS FROM THE SOIL was a simple process when it was mostly yellow ground which miners had to work. The gravels were loose and the diamonds readily visible. Even after the mining operations began to go deeper into the blueground, extraction was not very complicated. As was noted, the blueground was left to disintegrate in the air and the diamonds could then be picked out of the rubble.

But as the mines went deeper, it was discovered that the blueground took longer to weather and disintegrate naturally. Apparently, blueground became more resistant to air in relation to its depth. At some mines, it was taking up to a year for the blueground to dissolve sufficiently for diamonds to be extracted.

One thousand convicts were hired from the government by De Beers in the 1890's to sledge-hammer the blueground into workable chunks. Later, steam harrows were used to plough over the floors to pulverize the materials. Then came mechanical crushing machinery. Primary crushing procedures continue to be used in mining, but the process is carried out underground as a final stage before the ore is delivered to the treatment plant.

However, before the turn of the century, the crushed blueground was brought to a bed of "bullets." This was an apparatus in which a sieve was suspended in water. The entire structure was then rapidly shaken until the heavier elements of the deposit gradually sank between the bullets to the bottom. The lighter material floated to the top and was carried by the water over the edge of the sieve. This left the diamonds in the heavier material at the bottom of the sieve. Teams of trained workers then sifted through the resulting concentrate and retrieved the diamonds.

An employee of De Beers, F. B. Kirsten, in the mid-1890's, discovered that diamonds in the concentrate adhered to grease as the other minerals washed through. A sloping table with five steps was developed by De Beers' chief engineer, G. F. Labram. The top of this table was coated with a quarter inch of axle grease. A stream of water carrying the concentrate washed down the table as the grease trapped the diamond crystals passing over it. This process became the final step prior to sorting the crystals by hand and considerably reduced the labor of sorting crystals from the entire deposit.

The process has evolved into complex modern treatment plants which now subject materials to a series of concentrating processes which reject all materials except diamonds through washing, sorting gravels by size, sorting gravels by gravity, then extracting diamonds through further technical means. The final stage involves sorting crystals by hand. Although the process must be adapted to the individual demands of the particular mining operation, there are certain general stages through which all diamond mining passes.

Once the deposits are removed from the mine, the rock, or conglomerate in which the diamonds are held, must be crushed. Any crushing process, of course, must be carried out in such a way where the diamonds themselves are not broken apart. A similar process, involving milling rather than crushing, places the diamondiferous material in large rotating drums with water and rocks. The movement of the drums gradually breaks down the deposits and releases the crystals. A related principle is involved in scrubbing. This process is employed when an alluvial deposit is locked in hard clay. Scrubbing also involves tumbling the deposit in large drums through a washing action.

Washing is a vital step in the extraction of diamonds, because it removes the finer material brought up in the deposit. Usually, washing is combined with a screening process where the gravels are passed over a screen to remove particles of a particular size. The material to be discarded is allowed to pass through the screen. Depending on the size of the mesh in the screen, the discard can be thrown out with assurance that no diamonds worth retrieving are contained in it. The rejected material is known as "tailings."

The largest mesh screen—called a "grizzly"—consists of a row of widely spaced steel bars which separate large rocks that must be crushed prior to further processing. The finest screen allows only water and small sand particles to pass through.

There are many separating processes which mining companies have used over the years to extract diamonds from rough deposits. Some are complex, involving ferro-silicon powder suspended in water to a specific controlled density; some employ a centrifuge effect through an exact specific gravity. It is vitally important to understand the principle of separating diamonds from other deposits.

The grease table or grease belt is one method which has proven reliable in many mining operations, but not in all. The advantage of belts is that the process does not have to be stopped—as is the problem with the tables. Instead, the grease can be applied automatically and scraped off automatically while the diamonds adhere to it. The principle of the grease belt allows the concentrate to be fed across the belt with a strong flow of water. Diamonds trapped by the grease are taken across the flow of concentrate by the movement of the belt and scraped off by a heated scraper blade as the belt goes around the end of the roller.

However, not all diamonds will shed water and stick to grease. The diamonds from the marine terraces of South West Africa, for example, were washed over the grease; due to a sufficiently thick molecular salt coating on the crystals, they resisted the grease. Further research disclosed that the concentrate could be treated with fish acid oil and caustic soda. This enabled the diamonds to stick to the grease.

Another problem with the grease belt is that small diamonds will not adhere, even after treating the concentrate with a reagent. One solution to this problem was to put the concentrate through an "attrition mill" which ground down all minerals except diamond into a slime.

A process which has been perfected for use at several mining operations involves X-rays. The separation technique using the X-ray was announced in 1958 by the Russians who reportedly had developed the technique for new mines in Yakutia. The principle involved is that most diamonds fluoresce, or produce a lighting effect when subjected to radiation from an outside source. Nearly all the other minerals in the deposit do not behave in this manner. By passing the concentrate through the recovery machine and under an X-ray beam in an otherwise darkened environment, the diamond will light up, triggering a photoelectric cell. This cell causes a gate to open and the diamond is deflected into a separate chute.

The importance of accuracy in the recovery process is seen in the proportions of diamond to ore—thirty-five million to one. The loss of only a few crystals can mean the difference between profit and loss. Putting aside the possibility of total recovery (if indeed such a possibility is a reality even today), the mining company must face another fact of life: of the total world production of rough diamonds, only about twenty percent are suitable as gems. The remainder goes into industrial use.

Once the diamonds are recovered from the total deposit, they are sorted into one of several categories:

1. Stones—octahedral in shape with the appearance of four-sided pyramids joined at the bases.
2. Cleavages—broken pieces of block crystals.
3. Macles—triangular twinned stones.
4. Flats—thin flat diamonds possessing sufficient substance to be cut.

Stones which weigh less than one carat in the rough are known as "melee," while cleavages under one carat in the rough are called "chips." Other terms of importance are "bort," "ballas," and "carbonado." All of these are varieties of diamond used only in industry.

Before a diamond becomes the gemstone in a piece of jewelry, it undergoes a severe series of gradations which determine the quality and the value of the gem. In this process, diamonds suitable for industrial use are also determined.

A gem diamond undergoes a long process of sorting which involves the miners, the Diamond Trading Company, the cutter, the jewelry manufacturer, and the retailer. An industrial stone is sorted only in the early stages of processing.

The two terms, "sorting" and "grading," though they are related, are quite different. Once sorted, the stone is graded. Generally, sorting is a term used for crystals which are divided according to commercial characteristics. Grading is a term used more frequently with polished stones which undergo separation according to strict degrees of quality. Sorting and grading processes are carried out to determine the commercial value of diamonds.

Diamonds are classified, or separated into a large number of categories. There are at least a dozen, and these will vary from mine to mine. Some of the general features which determine classification are as follows: high quality crystals, known as "close goods," irregularities in crystallization, spotted stones, color and, perhaps, size. Very small crystals which wind up being passed through a fine sieve are separated and become known as sand. Diamonds are sorted by highly skilled individuals who can instantly identify subtle differences in crystals. They sit at benches in the central sorting offices at Kimberley before windows which face south and which stretch the length of the rooms. The benches at which they work are covered with fresh white paper. In London, where the diamonds undergo another sorting process, the room is similarly appointed, except that the windows face the north. There, the problem of the short daylight hours in the winter months limit the time during which diamonds can be sorted for color.

All gem diamonds initially are sorted into two general categories. The first group includes diamonds weighing more than a certain amount. This amount depends on the market; usually, however, the minimum weight is a carat. The second group includes the crystals under the cutoff weight; these crystals are considered "melee."

Sizes are determined through the sieving process—not in sorting. Professional sorters separate diamonds according to crystal forms, colors, and qualities. Although there are nearly a dozen different size groupings, four general categories —stones, cleavages, macles, and flats—provide an adequate overview of the practice. For definitions of these categories, see page 66.

When a sorter receives a group of crystals for separation, he looks first for the pure regular octahedra crystals known as stones. Next, he looks for any unbroken octahedra which may be irregular in form with varying degrees of inclusion. From that point, the sorter separates cleavages, then macles, and finally, the flats.

Once the entire pile of stones is separated in this general fashion, the sorter returns to each pile in order to divide the crystals according to quality. He must take special care at this point since this procedure will separate the stones for the cutter, who will go through his procedures according to the type of crystal he believes he has been given. For example, in this step of the sorting process, an octahedral crystal with a heavy inclusion near one point of the octahedron still will be classified as a clean crystal, because the corners will be bruted away during cutting. But a crystal with an inclusion near the center will be classified as one with low value, because a greater amount of stone will be lost during cutting. A well-shaped octahedral crystal with an inclusion at the center will undergo the loss of a substantial amount of crystal since so much of the material will have to be sawed away.

The sorter picks up a crystal between thumb and first finger and twists it with a rolling action, examining the entire stone, probably with a 6x hand lens, to determine its grade.

A scale of one to ten is used for grading the quality. Stones may be classified only according to the first five grades, although this may be extended to seven if the market demand is high. This becomes the gem group. The remainder—from five, six, or seven to ten—are of near-gem quality and merge into industrials. The scale is from one to four for cleavages, macles, and flats in the gem group, but this also may be extended to seven if the demand is sufficiently great.

When the crystals have been sorted, they are examined by the chief valuator, who prices the classified crystals. As you can imagine, such responsibility calls for a high degree of judgment based on long experience in the profession. A basic figure can be calculated according to a previous arrangement among diamond producers. Once that basic figure is reached, valuation depends on the flaws and the position of those flaws and their relation to value once the crystal is cut and finished; on color; and on size.

Finally, after the diamonds are re-sorted, they are classed according to weight. Crystals weighing more than 14.8 carats are sold separately. The rest are weighed to one-tenth of a carat, and the weight is shown to one decimal point, or 3.4 ct., 14.7 ct., etc.

The beauty of a gem diamond depends on the process which it undergoes before it reaches the retail market. Although its potential may lie, to a great degree, in its condition in the rough, the skill of the cutter, grinder, bruter, and polisher will determine the extent to which that potential is realized.

Early Indian cutters in the Middle Ages could only cut off the rough corners of a crystal, then laboriously polish the stone as best they could, either by rubbing diamonds together or by using abrasives softer than the diamond itself. Prior to 1475, this was about all that was done to a rough crystal. The process of reducing the diamond to dust, then using that dust to cut and polish facets into the gem, was a concept introduced by a Belgian lapidist, Ludwig van Berquen in 1475. Van Berquen also began designing diamonds according to facets, so light could enter as well as reflect back to the viewer according to the surfaces faceted into the stone.

The process of cleaving is a quick way to shape a diamond. It consists of splitting a stone into two or more parts to produce either a stone of better quality (such as cleaving off an inclusion) or produce a saleable stone more economically. Usually, octahedral forms are produced through cleaving—a result of the definite pattern of the crystalline mineral of the diamond.

More than likely, before cleaving was known to the diamond finishing trade, stones were ground and polished; the polishing, no doubt, was simply a refinement of the grinding.

Bruting is a process through which one diamond is shaped by another whole piece of diamond set in a stick, rather than through the use of diamond dust. Bruting precedes faceting. After bruting, sawing became the specialized form of grinding which divided diamond crystals in manufacturing.

Cleaving, or splitting, involves cutting a groove in the stone at the proper place, parallel to the cleavage or grain, or the pattern of crystalline formation on a rough diamond. A steel blade is placed in the groove and a sharp blow is struck, dividing the stone. Any fragments which result in the process drop into a box below the cleaving point. Cleaving can be done only *parallel* to a cleavage.

Sawing is a far slower and more tedious process and is used to halve an octahedral crystal into unequal parts near the middle, or widest portion. When sawed in this fashion, two diamonds emerge, but one is smaller than the other, and one has a table resulting from the process. Sawing is accomplished by the use of a paper-thin disc consisting of phosphor-bronze, spun at extremely high speeds.

Bruting is the process of rounding the corners of a diamond. At first, the process involved the use of a stone, called a "sharp," cemented to the end of a stick, which was used to rub the corners from a crystal cemented in another stick. The sticks were held, one in each hand, then vigorously rubbed over the cleaving box to catch any chips of diamond which might drop off. Only an approximately rounded crystal could be achieved at that time. In 1891, a Mr. D. Rodrigues obtained a British patent for a bruting machine driven by power. This was the type of machine which eventually came into use as a bruter.

Other tools used in finishing diamonds include the tang and dop. The tang, is literally a tool holder and is used to hold the dop while the diamond is being ground and polished. The dop holds the diamond which is to be worked. The diamond is fixed in a fairly large amount of plumber's solder in the cup. The solder is softened over a flame and the diamond is embedded into it in such a way that the exposed portion of the crystal is the part that is to be worked. A weight was sometimes placed on top of the tang to increase the pressure during the grinding. In the second half of this century, mechanical dops began to be used with clamps instead of solder. Also, quadrants to set the angles have been incorporated in some tangs. The clamped diamond in a mechanical dop can be turned with ease and speed to position the stone for grinding the facets. Turning a stone in a solder dop is a lengthy process. However, there is a disadvantage to the mechanical dop; a stone is more easily lost from a mechanical device than when it is imbedded and melted from solder.

Sawing never has been a speedy procedure. Although modern techniques have brought the process a long way from what it was (it took one full year to cut the 410-carat Regent diamond in half), it remains a careful and somewhat laborious operation.

In 1823 the saw used to cut diamonds was made of "a fine wire of brass or iron, attached to the two ends of a piece of cane or whalebone, the teeth being formed by the particles of diamond powder, which became embedded in the wire, as soon as it is applied to the line," according to the writings of John Mawe.

Shortly before the twentieth century, the circular diamond saw came into use. There is reference to a procedure using a circular saw in 1874, but it wasn't until about 1905 that the process gained much recognition. It is impossible to saw a diamond in the direction of the octahedra, because the diamond will cleave instead. Therefore, diamonds must be sawed either in the cubic, or dodecahedral, direction. Usually the saw is used to separate a diamond in half in order to produce the table through which the diamond is viewed as a gem. The procedure can take anywhere from one to three weeks, depending on the size of the diamond being cut.

People who work in diamond finishing are able to maintain banks of saws all working simultaneously. To an ear that is trained to hear every sound and to decipher its meaning, any fluctuation in the sound of one of scores of diamond saws in motion is recognized and treated according to the meaning. If one saw strikes a particular flaw, the trained and experienced operator will hear it immediately and know just what to do.

All diamonds which end up as gems in a piece of jewelry are not necessarily cut and finished in exactly the same way. Variations may be the result of the shape of the rough crystal or the artistic design of the gem manufacturer. Various cuts are produced according to these guidelines:

1. *The Point Cut:* This is believed to be the earliest known diamond cut. Pointed diamonds have angles which fall below those of the natural octahedron and these probably were fashioned into point cuts. Pointed stones are found in the diamond jewelry of the Middle Ages, and remained popular into the Renaissance period.

2. *The Table Cut:* This is an octahedron with the top point flattened to a square facet, known as the table. There were occasions when the lower point also was ground to make a smaller facet known as the "collet" or "culet." To give early table cuts a sense of design, the bottom cut was made about half the size of the top cut. This type of stone was known as an Indian-cut diamond, since they were produced in the Orient. A table cut was produced through bruting and polishing. It dominated the diamond-wearing fashions well into the seventeenth century. Although point stones remained common, many were recut as table stones.

3. *The Rose Cut:* Examples of rose-cut diamonds are the "Koh-i-Noor," cut prior to 1530, and the "Great Mogul." It is a cut as old as the table cut, but has a flat back and a domed and faceted front. Cutting a rose cut into a diamond depends largely on the shape of the rough crystal. Rose cuts were found suitable for flatter and thinner crystals. The cut is supposed to resemble an opening rose bud. But a gem so fashioned lacks much of the sparkle found in gems cut differently. Diamonds which have been faceted on all sides are a form of rose-cut gems. These are

known as briolettes, pendeloques, and beads.

4. *Faceted Octahedra:* Adding facets modified the table stones. At first, modification consisted of grinding and polishing the four edges of the table and the pavilion, which produced four extra narrow facets on the top and four more on the bottom. This improved both the brilliance and lustre of the gem. Later, facets were ground on the edges, leading to a more complex design. Even as facets were being added in this manner, the original octahedral crystal could easily be seen in the finished gem.

5. *The Mazarin Cut:* This particular cut has a total of thirty-four facets—seventeen above and seventeen below the girdle. It was one of the early faceted cuts and was named after Cardinal Mazarin of France. The Cardinal left his famed "Stancy" and "Mirror of Portugal" gems in his will to the French Crown, providing they become known as The Mazarin Diamonds. The seventeen facets above the girdle included those around the table, and those below included the cutlet.

6. *The Brilliant Cut:* "Brilliants" refer generally to diamonds faceted with rounded corners or "cushion outlines," as well as those having the more modern conical shapes with round outlines. No individual person is credited with inventing the brilliant cut, although Vincenzio Perruzzi, a seventeenth century Venetian lapidary, has lent his name to one of the faceted cuts. A waning interest in the classical lines of the table-cut gem, as well as new interest in technical innovation which led to a recutting of old diamonds in the 1700's, helped develop the brilliants. In the following century, cushion shapes began to be more common as English cutters leaned toward

thinner girdles on their gems and Dutch cutters stayed with the thicker cut. The thinner, girdled stones chip more often than not. The modern brilliant was the result of a theoretical treatise by Marcel Tolkowsky in 1914. Usually, angles of the pavilion to the girdle and the angle of the crown were determined by the octahedral crystal angles. However, a few cutters had been experimenting and found brilliance could be increased through the reduction of the angles. Tolkowsky introduced an ideal cut which encouraged the use of machine bruting to round the crystals; he used machines to saw a shape to the stone. The result was a brilliant with a round girdle, a style that became nearly universal.

7. *Other Brilliant Cuts:* Not only the conical or standard brilliants are known as brilliant cuts or shapes. There is an oval brilliant, heart-shaped brilliant, pear-shaped pendeloque, and a boat-shaped marquise, or navette cut—all of which are classed as brilliants; they are generally called "fancies."

8. *Faceted Girdles:* Very little light is reflected internally in a normal brilliant-cut diamond. This is because the girdle usually is left in its bruted condition. If a cutter is particularly concerned with high quality, faceting or polishing the girdle can be accomplished. One American designer and cutter, Louis H. Roselar, produces forty small facets around the girdle. But this does not necessarily increase brilliancy.

9. *Step and Square Cuts:* Pointed or bevelled corners characterize a step or trap cut. Often such diamonds are known as emerald cuts. However, this is not an ideal form of cutting since brilliance and lustre are lost naturally in the process. The cuts may vary

from square to a rather lengthy oblong shape. An octahedral crystal, lengthened in a particular direction, is more suitable for step cuts. There is a severe drawback to the emerald or square-cut diamond, and that is that it produces a window through which the viewer can look when viewing the stone from the table. To avoid windows, the pavilion facets should be cut at greater than critical angles (angles characteristic of the diamond which give it the ability to bend light), which is sometimes difficult, especially with the end pavilion facets of an elongated octahedral crystal.

The manner in which a particular diamond is cut depends completely on its optical properties. Since most of the prized diamonds have no color, there are other characteristics which, when brought out and highlighted through the finishing process, produces a beauty which make them prized stones. These additional qualities include a *high refractive index, a high degree of clarity, the ability to disperse color, brilliance, reflective ability, and lustre.* With these potentials in mind, a designer is confined by certain laws pertaining to optics.

Lustre is the quality of the light reflected from the surface of a material; in a diamond, this is known as "adamantine lustre" and is a quality unique to the stone. No other gems, with the possible exceptions of zircon and demantoid garnet, approach this quality. The ability to absorb a certain amount of light rays before reflection occurs, helps to determine the quality of lustre in a diamond. Diamond is the exception to the rule which holds that clear materials do not have reflective values. The surface of a diamond will reflect up to seventeen percent of the light to which it is directly exposed, compared to a reflection of about five percent in a transparent glass gem. This ability of the diamond can be illustrated with a diamond cut from a flat plate and observed by a stationary witness in motionless surroundings. Little lustre appears under such circumstances. But a diamond in a rose or brilliant cut, seen in moving candlelight, has a high degree of lustre.

"Brilliance" is the main purpose of diamond cutting. And brilliance is characterized by life and dispersion in a gem. Life is the amount of light which, after falling on a stone from the front, is reflected back to the viewer. Dispersion is the amount of color flashing caused by the stone splitting white light into the colors of the spectrum. Lustre is the end result of these qualities.

When these results are achieved, around eighty percent of the light entering a diamond does not pass through it, but instead is bounced back and forth within the gem to produce the desired effects. This depends on critical angles of the facets which end up acting like mirrors for the light coming into the diamond. Most of the light entering a diamond enters from the front, so it must be reflected out of the front and back to the viewer in order to achieve the maximum amount of life in the gem. The more the light is bent once it enters the stone (its refractive capabilities), the more dispersion is produced; the more the light is refracted, the more a gem's "life" is decreased. It is not possible to achieve maximum life and maximum dispersion at the same time.

The option, then, is to strike a balance between life and fire during the cutting process. The result is "brilliance," which also gives a diamond an almost "sharp" or "hard" appearance that is easily recognizable to those who handle diamonds with any regularity.

Although diamond "manufacturing" is an inappropriate term, it applies to any diamond process in which the gem is produced from the crystal. The cutter and the polisher are known to the diamond trade as "manufacturers." But the term is misused because literally, actual manufacturing is the process of producing synthetic diamonds. However, since the term applies to the process of finishing diamonds, it will be accepted for our purposes and applied, at this point, to the procedure of taking a diamond from rough crystal and making it into a gem.

There is a designer in each diamond factory who is often the owner of the cutting works himself. The job of a designer is both difficult and vital, for he must take a rough crystal and decide what is going to be done with it. He can't go back and retrace his mistakes or take back a decision to cut a stone a particular way once the tools have gone to work. If he has a clean, regular octahedra, the task is simplified greatly. But there are many large, irregular stones with no crystal faces and this complicates the process. When the Cullinan was discovered, it took weeks of studying before a decision was made to actually cut. Once a stone has been cleaved or sawed, decisions on polishing are relatively simple because the grain against which the polishing is done becomes clear.

Before that step becomes possible, however, a designer must consider the weight of the crystal and its quality (its obvious characteristics as well as its potential). A basic consideration is the minimum number of diamonds into which a crystal can be cut. Because the prices per carat increases considerably as the size of a stone increases, no designer cares to reduce the profit through extra cutting procedures which result in loss of carat weight through the accumulation of dust.

Then there is the question of demand on the current market. Any market demand can fluctuate and the market controlling diamonds is no different. At times, certain cuts and sizes are more popular than others; lower qualities of rough crystal can become either low-quality gems or industrial diamonds. This is all a question of market demand.

There are properties inherent in the stone which must be considered in the initial design process, such as whether it is a "stone," a "shape," a "cleavage," a "macle," or a "flat"; whether it is coated or not; and the actual shape of the crystal, which ultimately determines how it can be cut, and the resulting shape of the cut diamonds. An example of shape is seen in a well-shaped octahedron which, if small, becomes one brilliant, or two brilliants, if large enough. But an elongated octahedron may be cut into a brilliant-cut oval or marquise, or an emerald-cut diamond, if the quality is high. A large irregular crystal might become polished stones of various cuts. The "cut" as a term, describes the shape of the finished diamond and the pattern of the facets. The "brilliant" is the standard for the diamond and the rest are lumped together under the term, "fancy cuts."

The "make" of a diamond refers to the finished brilliant's proximity to ideal proportions. A stone which approximates the ideal is said to be a "good" or "fine" make. One that has been cut in order to gain weight; or to spread the diameter making it weigh less than it should; or is "out of round;" or has the pavilion "out of center"; or has a girdle that is too thick; or has facets at incorrect angles; these are termed "poor," or "bad make."

Cutting considerations also work according to the market. If the cutter is working to produce medium and lower quality gems, a high return on the rough will be his primary goal. This can be accomplished by increasing the diameter of the stone through sacrificing some of the crown height and adding width to the table. As much as ten percent of the weight can be saved by spreading a stone instead of cutting it to ideal proportions.

Increasing the pavilion angles also causes a loss in

weight. A thick girdle will increase the weight considerably. Leaving a stone thick, in this manner, saves a great amount of weight.

Macles are a case in point if depth is needed; when they are cut as brilliants, they often turn out too thin to provide full depth without loss of too much material. Weight loss can be compensated for by increasing the girdle width and the culet size, as well as by spreading the table. Thin macles and flats become baguettes and other thin types of cuts.

If the rough crystal is too flat to become a reasonably acceptable brilliant, and too thick to be wasted on minor cuts, it is manufactured into a pear-shaped or marquise-cut diamond in which shallow pavilions are cut.

These, then, are the possibilities facing a designer when he first sees a rough crystal. It is not surprising that he takes a great deal of time to consider the destiny of a particular stone before allowing it to go to the tools. He can make an initial decision when he observes the position of the girdle. The thinnest side becomes the table and the thickest side the bottom. Inclusions preferably are kept near the top, as those in the bottom will be reflected several times and therefore appear magnified to the viewer. Once the girdle decision is made, he must examine the inside of the stone.

In order to see inside the crystal, the designer uses an 8X or 10X hand lens. He must imagine himself inside the stone, observing all the flaws and deciding which can be removed, which can be left in, and which can be polished out. Optimum value usually is achieved by maintaining a balance. To further determine the inside characteristics of a crystal, the designer will "open" the stone by grinding facets or even cleaving thin pieces off opposite faces. These become windows which he can peer through with his lens in order to get an accurate evaluation of the stone's potential.

Three general methods of manufacture are available to the designer: (1) makeables, or whole stones which are ground with no preliminary work such as macles, cleavages, chips, etc.; (2) sawed crystals, or stones, shapes, melee, chips, smalls, etc.; and (3) cleaved, such as cleavages, macles, chips, etc. When an approach has been decided upon, a mark on the crystal is made with a pen and Indian ink, using fine lines to mark the point where it is to be sawed or cleaved.

When a diamond cutter begins working on a crystal, all his considerations must relate to the grain of the stone. When he cleaves, he cleaves according to the grain; when he saws, he saws the grain; and when he polishes, he polishes the grain.

Cleaving follows the grain. The cleaver has at his disposal several sticks, each about eight inches long, and a cleaving box. The box, rectangular in shape, is attached to the work bench. There are hollows in the box to hold loose crystals. The stone to be cleaved is cemented to the end of one of the sticks with a special adhesive, basically a mixture of shellac and rosin with brick dust, finely powdered glass, or a similar material. A second diamond is cemented to another stick. This usually is a chip with a cleavage edge. It is used to nick the first diamond—the one to be cleaved— by marking a "kerf" on the inked line drawn by the designer. The kerf is produced by rubbing one diamond against the other; the chips which are removed fall into the cleaver's box. The diamond to be cleaved is then fixed upright in a tapered hole in the bench or in the box. A special blade is placed in the kerf and tapped with the handle end of a cleaver's stick. Sometimes a short iron bar is used as the hammer. The stone splits according to the cleavage plane. But to accomplish the task properly, a cleaver must possess a knowledge of diamond graining, have an eye which can perceive the cleavage before it is made, and maintain a steady hand that doesn't waver when the blow is made. Bad cleaving can shatter an otherwise high-quality diamond, simply by the action of the hammer tap.

A diamond is sawed in the direction opposite the cleavage. The workman who saws diamonds, actually "saws grain." If a natural girdle exists on an octahedron, it is usually that point through which the saw is made, dividing the crystal in two relatively equal parts. Diamond saws are very thin discs made of a special bronze, and the diameter of the disc is between three and four inches; the thickness, however, is only 0.06 to 0.15 mm. The RPM's of a moving diamond saw vary from 4,500 to 6,500, according to the needs of the particular situation. A central hole with several slots are cut into the blade to prevent it from bending into a concave during the sawing process. Diamond powder is made into a paste and then applied by hand to the disc.

The diamond to be sawed is mounted in a holder at the end of an arm of the machine. The saw blade rests below the stone. Gravity is the force which holds the diamond against the edge of the disc. But the weight or pressure is adjustable, since different crystals demand various pressures. A single disc will be used to cut about six one-carat stones. After this, it will have been worn too small for further use.

Within diamond crystals are degrees of hardness which can turn the blade and spoil a cut. To avoid this, the person in charge of the bank of saws must maintain careful watch over the diamonds as they are in the process of being cut. If a blade runs into a naat, or different degrees of hardness, the diamond may be sawed by a change in the direction of rotation, simply by crossing the machine's driving belt. Occasionally, a blade will wander toward a cleavage plane—or take the easy way out. When this happens, the stone is turned and the blade begins cutting from the opposite side.

Sawing is a laborious, slow process. Even with modern machinery and technology, it still takes about forty minutes to saw through a quarter-carat octahedral crystal.

Bruting is another finishing process used to shape a crystal. The stones are shaped according to circular outlines and can either be bruted after sawing or cleaving is accomplished, or on a whole stone, before sawing or cleaving. Bruting or grinding shapes the girdle of a diamond, or even creates a flat surface such as the table of a brilliant.

A bruting machine is similar to a wood lathe. The diamond is cemented into a dop which is mounted in the chuck of the machine. Another diamond, chosen as the tip of the cutting tool, is cemented to a similar dop at the end of a stick about two feet long. This stick is held under the bruter's arm and the diamond at the end is used to work the diamond that is to be shaped. Of course, it is necessary to keep the diamond that is being worked on a steady plane to avoid an out-of-round result. An oval may result, even when a circular effect is desired, unless the bruter is both skillful and careful.

Finally, the gem diamond is ground and polished. Grinding cuts in the facets of the stone, and polishing simply finishes what grinding begins.

A cast-iron disc, ten to twelve inches in diameter and about an inch thick when new, is used for grinding, and is called a "scaife." A steel axle with pointed ends runs through the center of the scaife so that the whole device looks like a large top. Surfaced with diamond paste, it grinds the diamonds and fashions the facets. The revolutions per minute of a rotating scaife total 2,500. The diamond being ground is in a holder fixed to a tang which is suspended over the surface of the scaife. One scaife can handle two to four diamonds at once; occasionally, it can service more. Three rings are placed on each scaife. The inner two are used for grinding, the outer ring for polishing. When the diamonds are running well, there is little noise in the process. A faint ringing is about the only sound that is audible. This indicates to the machine operator that the direction of the grind or polishing process is good. Occasionally, a stone will produce a loud ring even when it is running well, but this is the exception, not the rule.

There are steps to grinding and polishing which involve placing the facets on a stone. The first eighteen facets are ground by a "cross-cutter." These include the table, the culet, four corners, and four bezels on the top, and four corners and four pavilions on the bottom. The table is ground first; the next step is to grind a facet. At this point, the procedure becomes critical, because the accuracy of that first facet will determine the entire symmetry, life, fire, and ultimate quality of the finished gem.

Usually, the first facet is ground at a corner of the top of the stone. Although a gauge will be used to size the facet, judgment and skill, together with a lot of experience, also help determine a successful outcome. Next comes the opposite corner, and then the third and fourth facets are ground. Step by step, four facets are fashioned on top, four on the bottom; four more on the top, four on the bottom; four more on the top, four more on the bottom, and so forth until fifty-eight have been cut into the stone.

Finally, each quality diamond is given a final visual check known as "making over." This involves polishing very tiny facets and it does not affect the quality of the make to remove any small defects which may remain. Sometimes an acid bath completes the process of removing any oil or debris that may have collected in the tiny fractures which still exist.

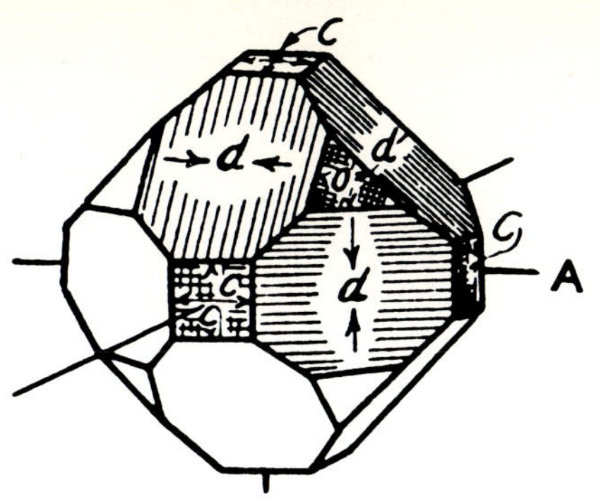

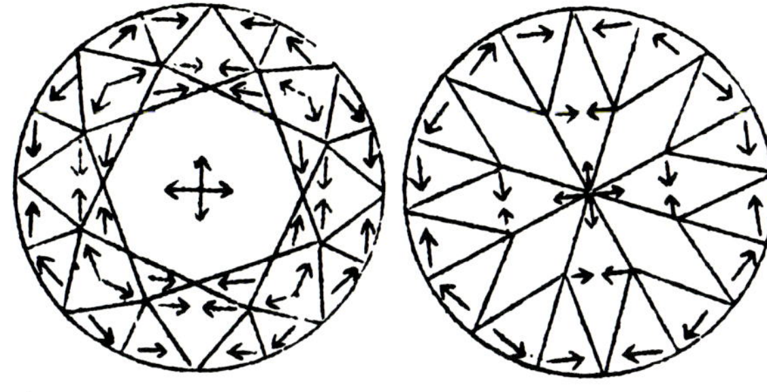

Polishing directions
on a diamond.
(*Courtesy Gemological
Institute of America*)

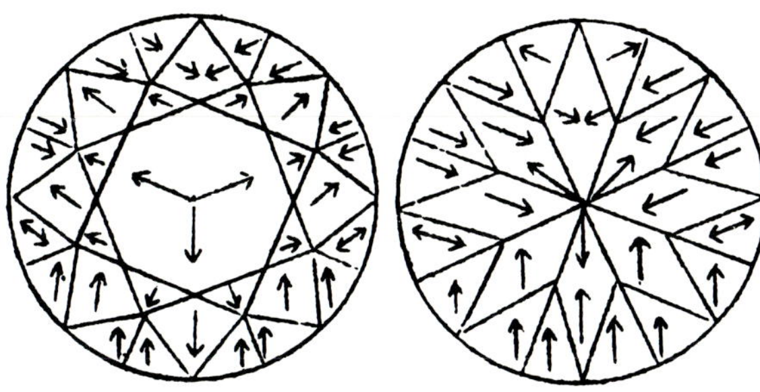

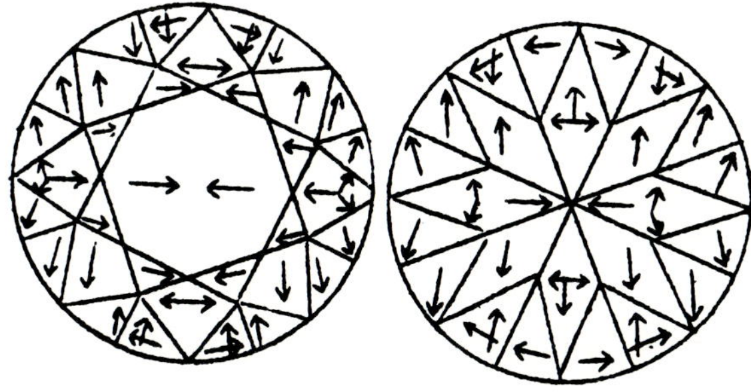

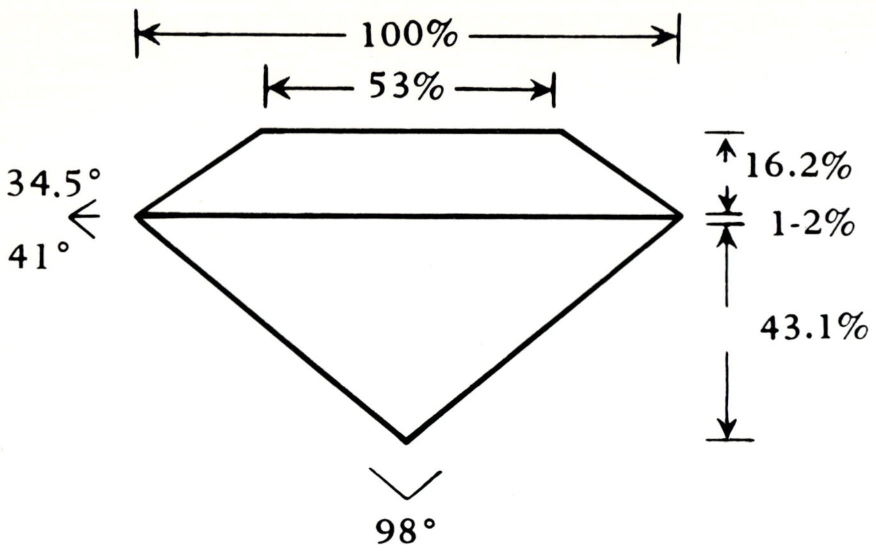

A properly cut and proportioned gem: American cut.
(*Courtesy Gemological Institute of America*)

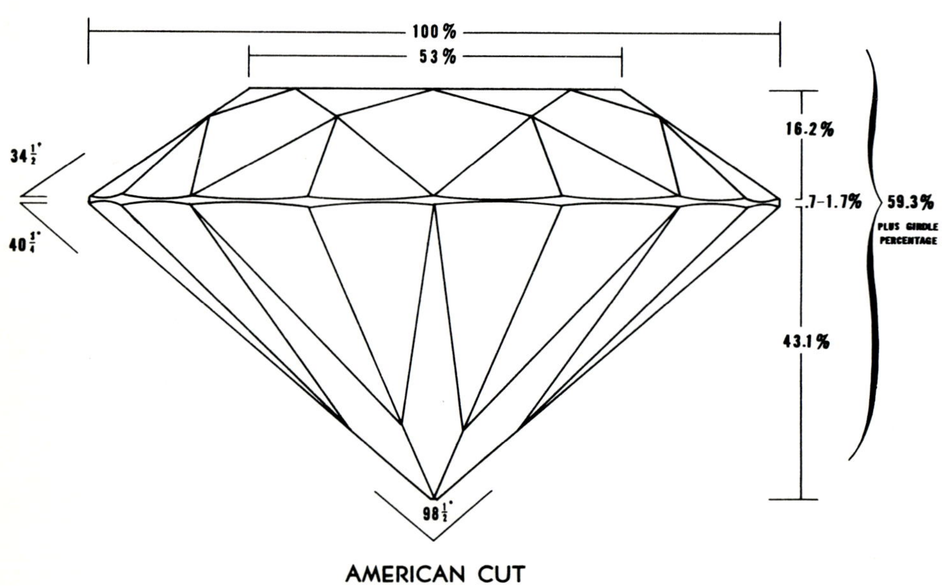

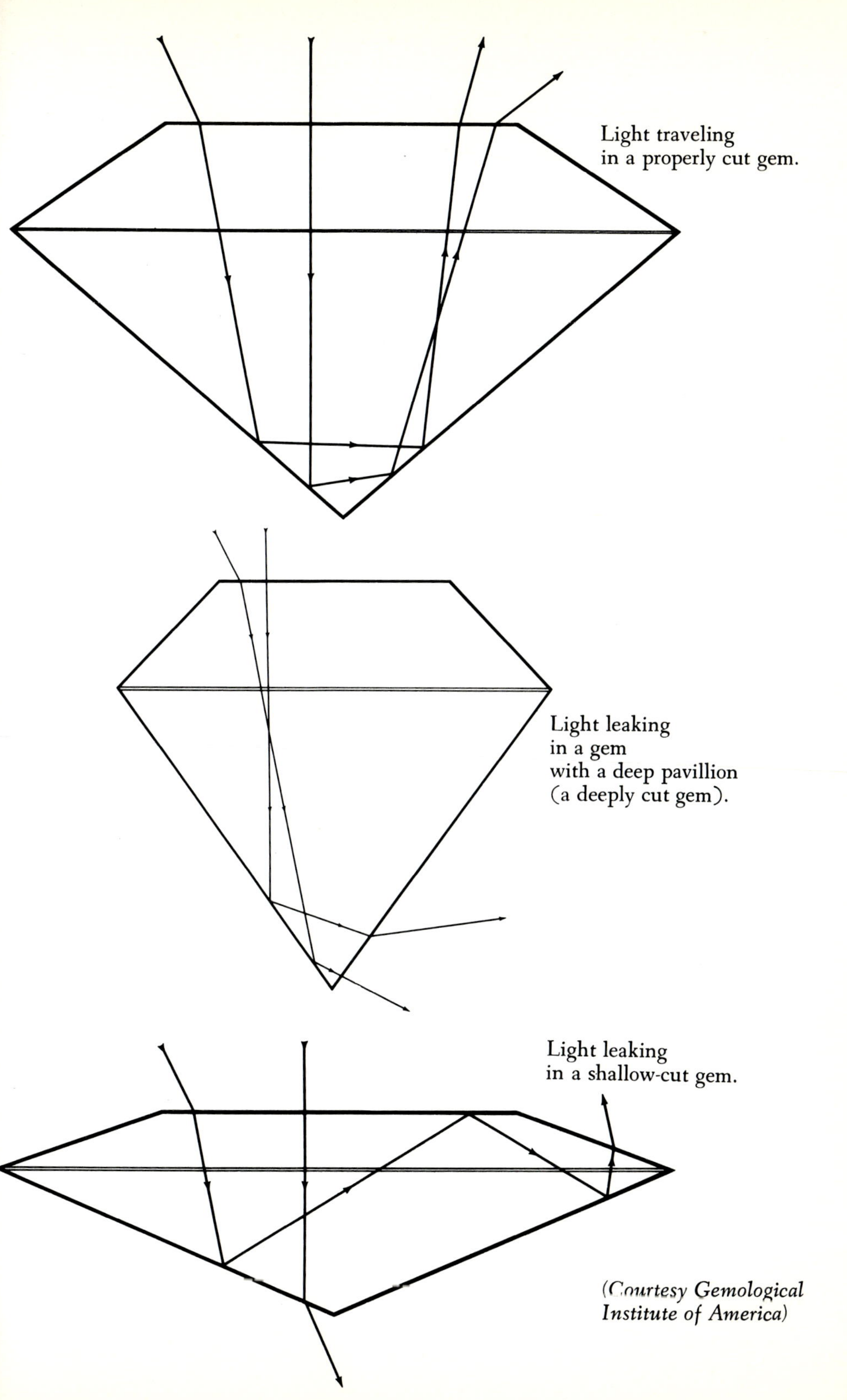

Light traveling
in a properly cut gem.

Light leaking
in a gem
with a deep pavillion
(a deeply cut gem).

Light leaking
in a shallow-cut gem.

(Courtesy Gemological
Institute of America)

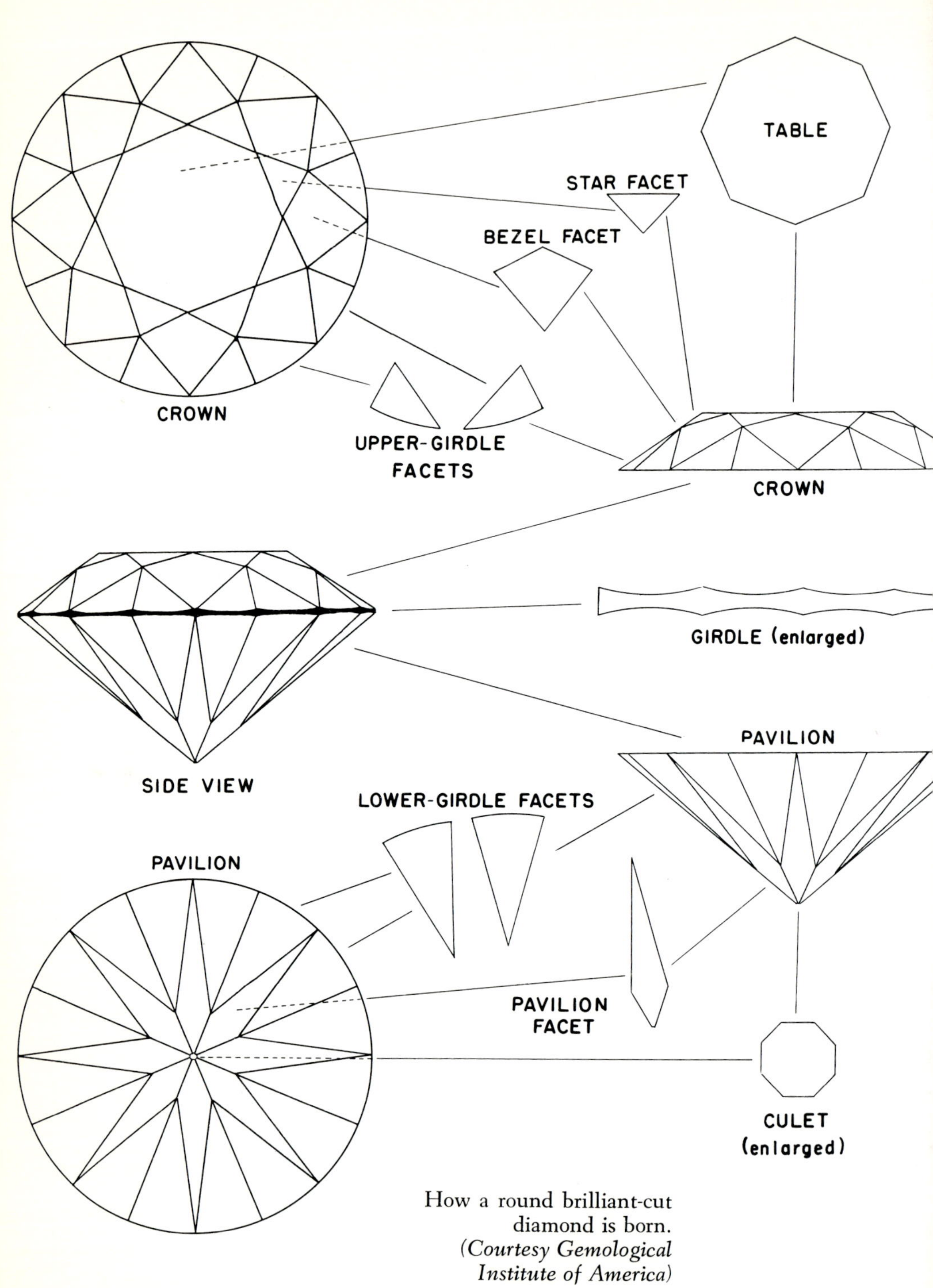

How a round brilliant-cut
diamond is born.
*(Courtesy Gemological
Institute of America)*

84d

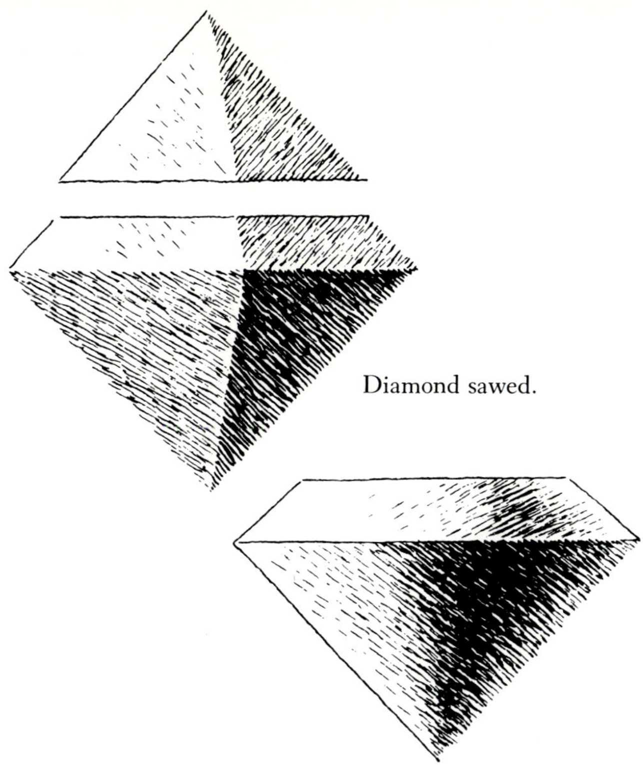

Diamond sawed.

*(Courtesy Gemological
Institute of America)*

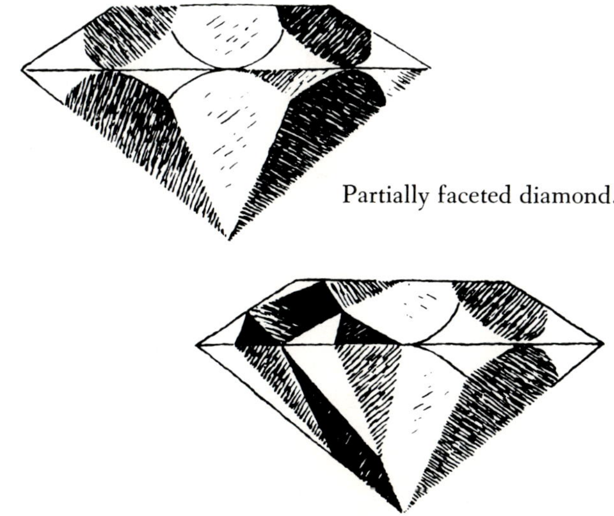

Partially faceted diamond.

POPULAR CUT DIAMONDS
(Courtesy N. W. Ayer & Son, Inc.)

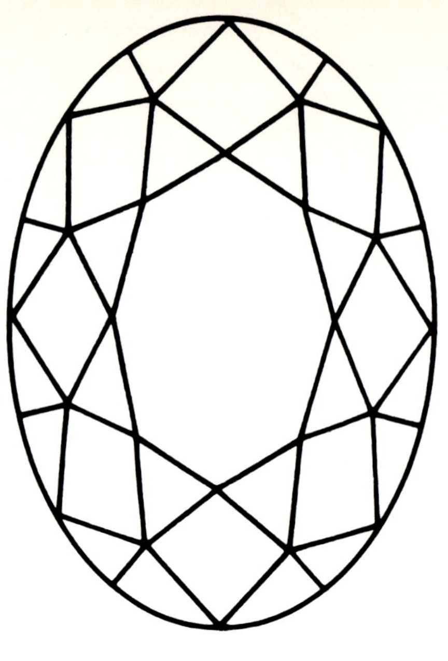

Oval.

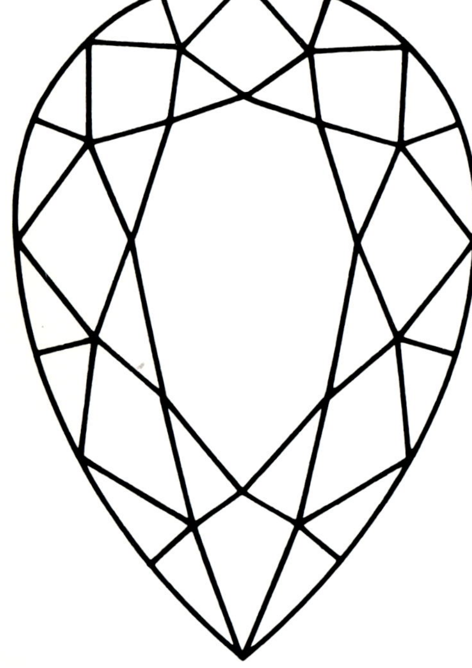

Marquise.

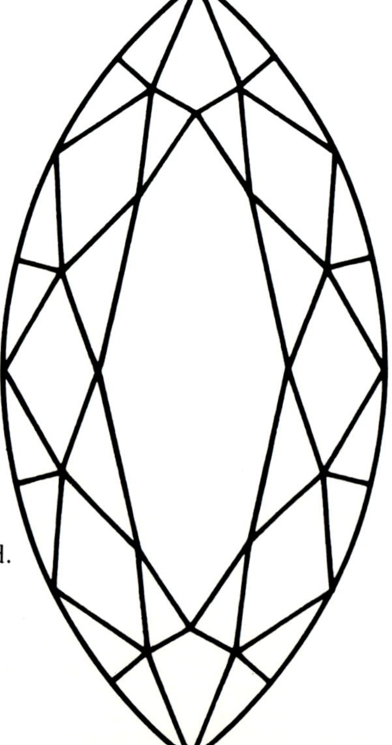

Pear-shaped.

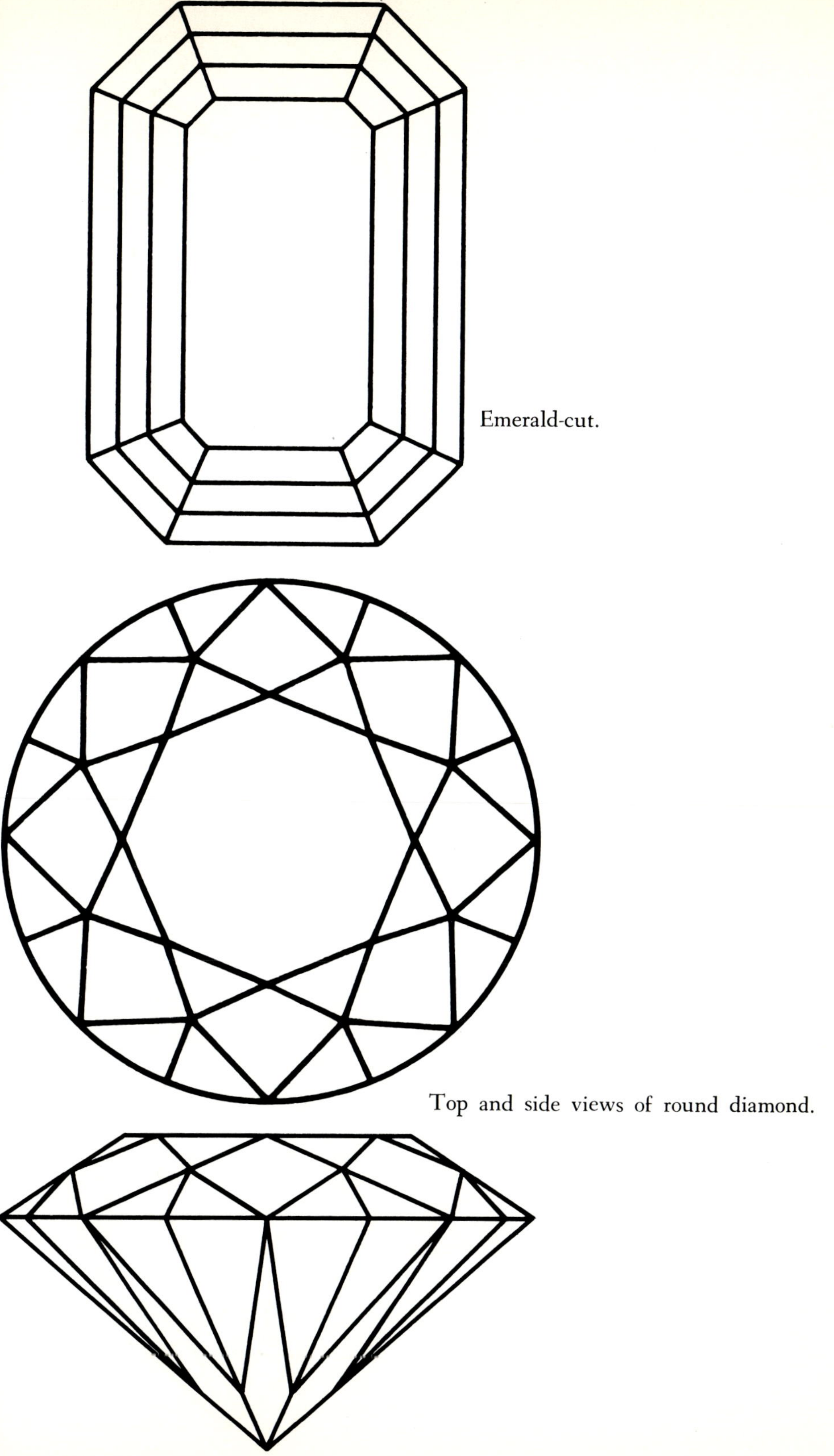

Emerald-cut.

Top and side views of round diamond.

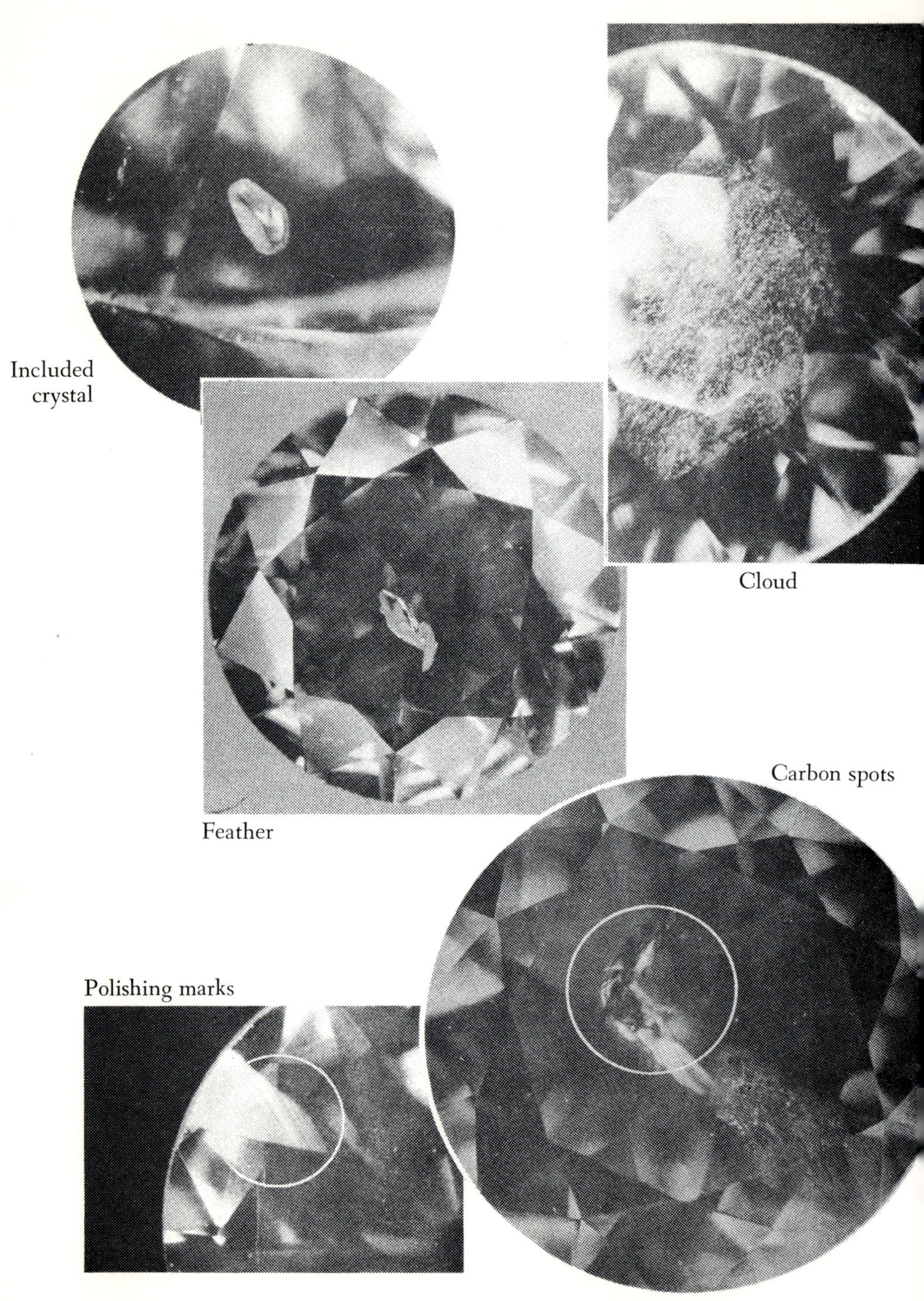
Included
crystal
Cloud
Feather
Carbon spots
Polishing marks

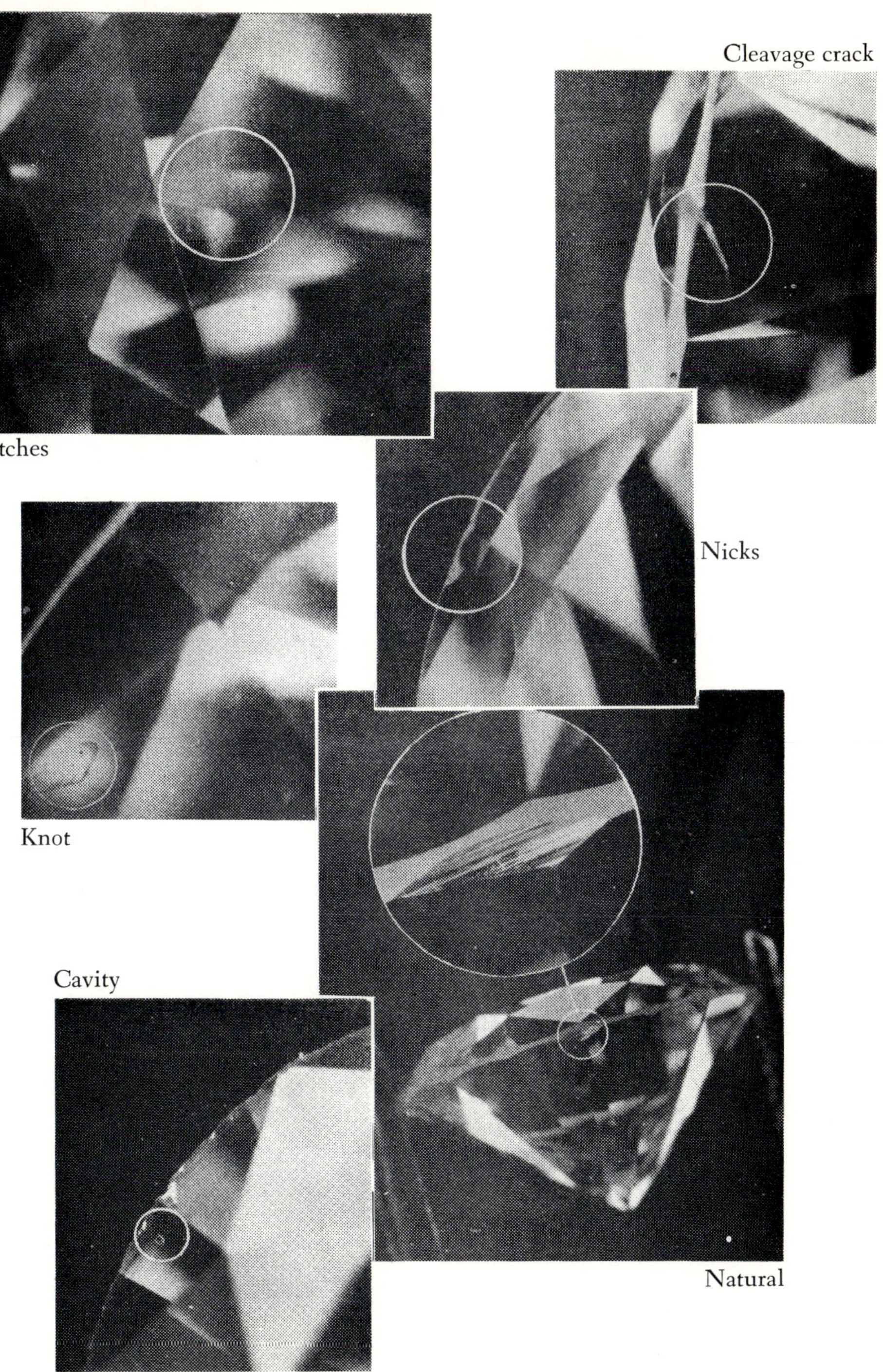
Cleavage crack
Scratches
Nicks
Knot
Cavity
Natural

COMPARISON OF THREE DIFFERENT DIAMOND COLOR-GRADING SYSTEMS

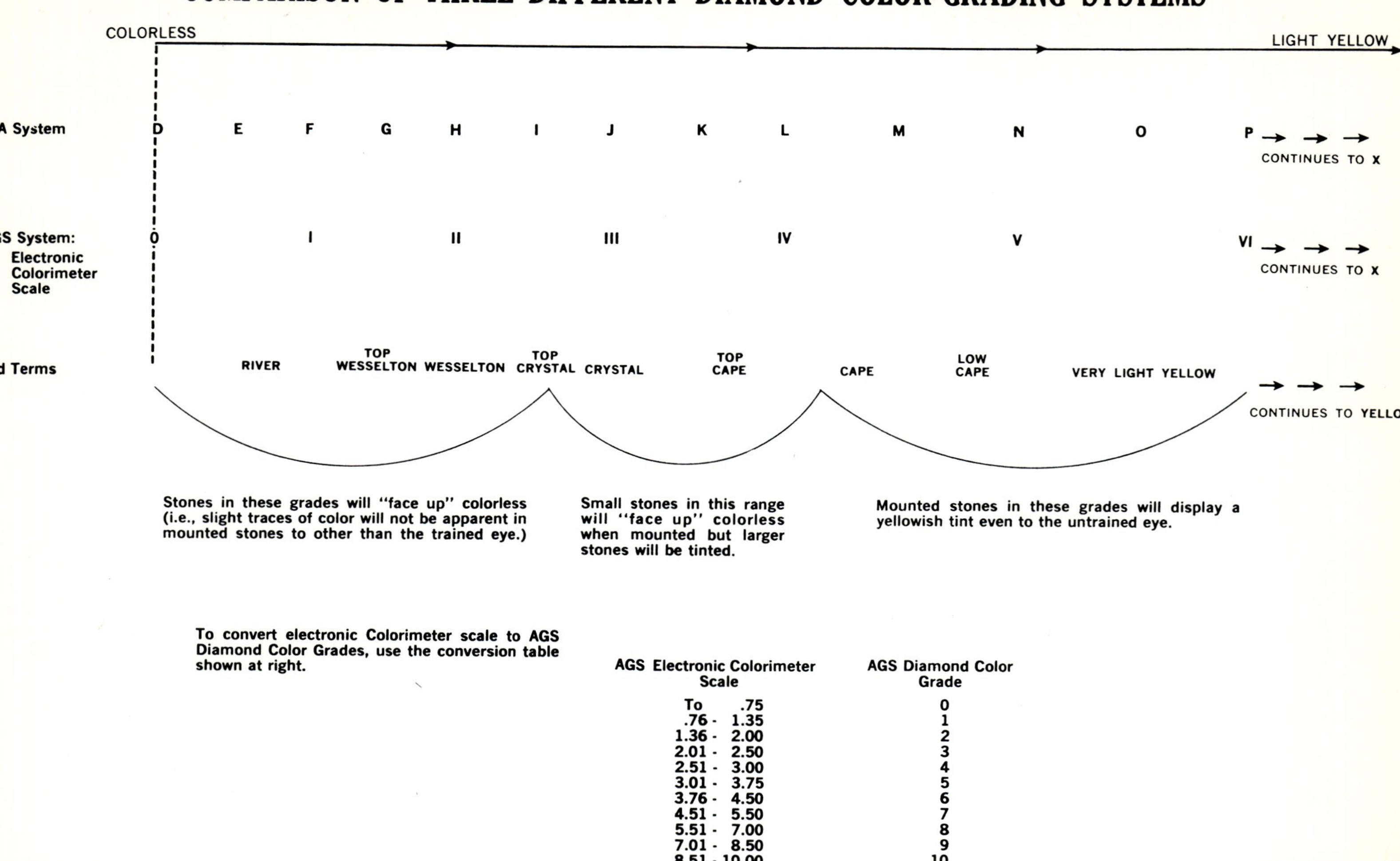

AGS Electronic Colorimeter Scale	AGS Diamond Color Grade
To .75	0
.76 - 1.35	1
1.36 - 2.00	2
2.01 - 2.50	3
2.51 - 3.00	4
3.01 - 3.75	5
3.76 - 4.50	6
4.51 - 5.50	7
5.51 - 7.00	8
7.01 - 8.50	9
8.51 - 10.00	10

Man-Made diamonds serve space-age industry. *Above:* A high-pressure-high-temperature press used to compress the tiny crystals of Borazon CBN is prepared for use. *Below:* A technician holds a cutting-tool insert fabricated from GE's Borazon CBN (Man-Made) diamond crystals, second in hardness only to natural diamond. (*Courtesy General Electric Co.*)

Above: A three-quarter-carat diamond created by scientists at the General Electric Research and Development Center, Schenectady, New York. The diamond has undergone slight polishing but has not been cut, so it retains the shape in which it was "grown" from graphite (the pile of black powder in the photograph—and the same stuff that is used in "lead" pencils) under extreme pressures and temperatures. *Below:* A handful of high-quality Man-Made diamonds (produced in a variety of colors as well as white) that, like the stone above, have also undergone slight polishing but have not been cut. (*Courtesy General Electric Co.*)

CHAPTER 7

The Grading and Valuation of Polished Diamonds

THE PROCESS OF BRINGING DIAMONDS from mine to market is so lengthy, involved, and intricate that it is understandable why the prices for finished stones are so high. But "high" is a relative term, and placed into the perspective of the mine-to-market process, the ultimate purchaser is getting his money's worth.

Even though diamonds have been traced from their origin as rough crystals coming from the earth, then moving into the hands of the designer, cutter, grinder, and polisher, the process is far from over. A polished gem—the ultimate results of the finisher—is not ready for market until it has been graded and a valuation placed on it.

Highest price per carat is based on how accurately proportioned the finished gem is when it comes from the finishing process. If a stone has been cut to gain weight, or has been spread to give a larger appearance, a shallowness or excessive depth may occur above or below the girdle. Perhaps, the table may be too wide in proportion to the total diameter of the gem. These are factors which will lower the per-carat price of the stone.

Often the naked eye can detect whether or not a stone is badly cut. However, a 10X lens instantly reveals the general degree of the cut. Lowest on the price scale are gems which have been cut badly—unsymmetrical, out-of-round, irregular tables, or misplaced facets all are characteristics of poorly finished stones. By examining the full diameter across the girdle, certain criteria can be used to determine the general grade of the stone. These criteria include the diameter of the table as a percentage of the full diameter; the height of the crown; the depth of the pavilion; and the thickness of the girdle.

If the table is too large in relation to the diameter of the stone, the crown's thickness is reduced. However, the angle may still remain correct. A shallow crown and a wide table result in smaller crown facets and a lesser display of the color spectrum. The crown facets are responsible for the fire of a prism revealed in a diamond. Also, when the crown is thin the pavilion will appear to be oversized. Yet, when placed in relation to the diameter of the stone itself, it may be reasonably correct.

If a stone is properly proportioned, a bright image of the table is revealed when the center of the table is viewed. The image of the table is brightened by reflections from the pavilion facets. When a diamond is too shallow below the girdle, a circular reflection can be seen near the table edges. This is a reflection of the girdle and is known to the trade as a "fisheye" or "cod's eye."

The next step in determining grade is to view the pavilion from a side angle. Modern gems are cut with long, lower girdle facets. The girdle itself should be neither too thin nor too thick. There may be small naturals on a girdle, but unless these extend over a facet they are not considered to be cutting flaws.

All facets on a gem diamond should be highly polished. There should be no interference in visible color by poor polishing. Occasionally, facets will be added to eliminate a damaged part of a crystal. If these are not large; they are acceptable to the market.

An "optical comparator" was introduced by the Gemological Institute of America in 1967 to determine the proportions of a brilliant in a short amount of time. It can handle diamonds up to eight carats. Basically, the optical comparator magnifies the shadow of a stone by casting the shadow of a line diagram of correct proportions onto a screen. The stone under examination can then be compared with the correct proportions to determine relative accuracy in the finishing process.

The importance of proportion to per-carat price depends on the market. Currently, the American market is most conscious of proper proportion.

Diamond weight is described in carats. Carat weight was originally the seed of a tree common to the Middle East; it was known as the locust tree, or Carob tree. The fruit of this tree is a bean nearly black in color. A sweet syrup is found inside the pod along with several small seeds. Ancient pearl merchants from the Middle East discovered that the seeds were uniform in weight when dried; they were used to determine units of weight for pearls.

As various countries adopted the carat as gemstone weight, it was standardized according to their individual units of weight; these varied in each country. Early in this century, several nations agreed to accept an international standard metric carat which was one-fifth or 0.2 of a gram. It was also agreed that weights would be expressed in decimals instead of the previous fractions of 64ths. For example, under the previous system, weight would be shown in print as 12 36/64.

For informational purposes, there are several gauges which are used to determine weight: the hole gauge, the sieve, the Moe gauge, the Leveridge gauge, and weight determination according to a formula.

Pricing of diamonds (fixing valuations) is determined by a general guide which involves the square of the gem's weight. This is based on the guide written in 1750 by David Jeffries who held, "The . . . rule is that the proportional increase, or value of diamonds, is as the square of their weight, whether rough or manufactured." Today this rule has only general application, since the formula used is quite complex.

Since at least half the weight of a stone is lost in manufacturing, the price more than doubles for the polished gem in comparison to the rough crystal from which it was made. And this does not include the costs of finishing. Using this general guide, a two-carat rough crystal, finished into a one-carat gem diamond, has about the same value. If a regular purchaser of diamonds is evaluating a particular group of gems, he probably has the current price structure fixed in his mind. For those who do not handle diamonds regularly on the market, three general rules can be adopted to arrive at a fairly accurate valuation: (1) weigh the stone or accurately estimate the weight by a gauge, preferably a Leveridge gauge; (2) evaluate the quality of the stone by color, clarity, and cut; and (3) refer to a price chart.

The third rule is usually the stumbling block. Usually the so-called "four C's" are used to determine price or value: carat weight, color, clarity, and cut. The first, of course, refers to size; the others refer to quality. Since the combinations of these four criteria vary almost infinitely, pricing is a complex procedure. Combine these factors with the rare occurrence of diamonds, the durability of the gemstone; the fact that it never wears out, the fact that it needs no maintenance, its fame as a symbol of love and affection, its popularity as a symbol of wealth, and you have all the ingredients for a complex pricing structure. Yet one has been devised. Actual buying and selling information undoubtedly is the most useful in determining the price of a particular stone, but a personal chart can be compiled on the basis of weight, color, clarity, and cut.

The most important factor on this chart is, without a doubt, the weight factor; it should be listed separately. Assuming that all gems are of good cut, and grouping color and quality, a chart can be compiled in which weights comprise one coordinate, and the quality factors the other.

Since fine grading of nuances and minute differences in stones are not among the purposes of this chart, only the middle grades on a broad scale need be considered.

The continual upward trend in prices must be kept in mind. Although major price changes occur when the prices of rough crystals increase, a five percent rise at the mine does not mean a five percent rise at the retail market level. The increase is an average one to cutters and more than likely will increase the price of higher quality stones at the expense of lower quality goods.

At times, a heavy demand for a particular type of cut stone will occur. This means that there will be sharp rises and falls in any curve drawn to trace the diamond market.

Public attitude toward a particular type of gem also influences market price. Color and clarity influence price to almost the same extent, but even this is misleading, for the actual demand depends on public wishes. There are regions in the world where color may be deficient in a gem diamond, but if the cut is flawless it will bring a good market price. In other parts of the world, the reverse may be true.

Although most diamonds are transparent (the so-called "white diamonds"), those with a tinge of color seem to be acceptable because of a certain warmth that radiates with the color. Few diamonds are icy white, or totally colorless, because even a small amount of color can be perceived when a stone is viewed through the side, especially with a 10X lens, or loupe. Most diamonds reveal shades of yellow or brown, with some bearing shades of pink, orange, green, and blue. These colored diamonds are known as "fancies" and are valued for their rarity. The deeper colors possess incomparable beauty, but do not reflect the brilliance of the lighter colors.

Tiny bubbles of uncrystallized carbon, hairlines, or feathers, form inclusions in gems which influence the clarity of a stone. Those which cannot be cleaved, sawed, ground, or polished out in the finishing process interfere with the passage of light through the stone and therefore influence quality; and quality influences price.

Most (in fact, nearly all) diamonds are precision cuts. If careful examination reveals that a stone has less brilliance and fire than another of comparable size, the reason is a poor finishing job. Through close study, it is possible to see that the less fiery diamond has facet angles and proportions which do not match those of the stone with the superior fire and brilliance.

A general fact to remember is that diamonds of comparable quality vary in price only because of size. Size is the main consideration, since the finishing process on a smaller diamond is just as exact as on a larger one.

Diamonds are a good investment, providing a particular stone remains marketable. If a gem is being purchased as an "investment" by the customer at the retail level, he must keep in mind that a diamond which cannot be moved back onto the market in an emergency loses its investment value. However, gem diamonds—especially when set in jewelry—become objects of beauty, prized for reasons other than "investment."

Owning a high-quality solitaire diamond ring may turn out to mean little if that jeweled piece is exchanged for a high-quality sports car which decreases drastically in value in four to five years. The ring retains the same value as it always had.

So a diamond undoubtedly has its own inherent "purchasing power." But since it is a rare "gem among gems," it retains its power while nearly all other material possessions inherently decrease in value.

Because the diamond market remains relatively stable, with ample notification of any price changes, and because the standards of diamond quality are universal and can be determined in any gemstone, an appraisal of diamonds and diamond jewelry is, more or less, an accurate process.

This is still relative, however. There are always fluctuations in any market, and an appraisal of a diamond is made on the assumption that the price quoted is one which the market will bear for that particular stone at that particular time. Since markets vary according to the country involved, appraisals also must take this into consideration.

Then there is the operation of controls placed on the diamond market from what might be called the "syndicate." Without the economic and even social overtones which often accompany the term, a syndicate is nothing more than an association of individuals who perform official business by combining their efforts to carry out a particular transaction. This aptly describes the association which works to control the diamond market and keep it from peaking and dipping according to a demand which cannot be fulfilled by supply or a supply which is too far on the surplus side. It is known as the "Diamond Producers' Association" and it formulates diamond policy and sets quotas. Included in its membership is the De Beers group in South and South West Africa; the Diamond Corporation, which is a De Beers subsidiary; and the South African Government which is considered a producer because of its ownership of the state diggings in Namaqualand. The Association makes marketing agreements with outside producers through the Diamond Corporation.

This, then, is the association which works to control the market. There is another corporation known as the Diamond Trading Company, formed in 1934, which actually sells the diamonds. This company, along with the Diamond Producers' Association, forms the basic operation known as the Central Selling Organization. The CSO is a group of marketing companies which handle all the sales for the principal diamond producers on a cooperative basis. All diamonds processed through the CSO are sent by the mines to the DPA offices in Johannesburg or the offices of the Diamond Corporation in London. There they are divided into gem and industrial diamonds and sold through separate channels.

Gems are sold through the Diamond Purchasing and Trading Company to the Diamond Trading Company. The DTC sorts them into separate parcels which are offered at sales, or "sights" held ten times each year. Some eighty percent of the world's gem diamonds are marketed in this fashion.

The manner in which the market is controlled depends on the demand and how this demand is exercised at the sights. During the 1960's, demand increased to such an extent that buyers at the sights were able to resell at ever-increasing prices. If the situation evolves in which buyers generally are reluctant to take goods they know cannot be resold for profit, however, the CSO will stockpile the stones and maintain its prices through this action. Nonetheless, the CSO does sell all the diamonds that the market can absorb.

If demands fall off drastically, the producers' association can allocate sales quotas to each of its members and also instruct the Diamond Corporation to limit its purchases from producers who have agreements with the association. There have been occasions when a trade depression became severe enough to warrant closing mines. When this occurred, the CSO simply stockpiled stones while mining operations continued according to the desires of the producers. When the demand was low, there naturally was a curtailing of mining operations since it just isn't good business to over-stock a market in which there is a reduced demand for the product.

In 1963, when the emerging African states objected to trading with companies operating from South Africa, a re-organization of the Central Selling Organization became necessary. The result of this was that purchasing operations in some countries were transferred to the Diamond Corporation. The Diamond Corporation of West Africa Limited, for example, buys all the production of individual diggers and a large portion of production from the Sierra Leone Selection Trust. Additionally, there are separate purchasing arrangements in effect in the Congo and Angola.

Alternative arrangements also were made with Russia in 1963 because of the Soviet trade boycott of South Africa. An agreement had been made in 1959 between De Beers and the Soviets to market Russian stones through the CSO. The special arrangements became necessary when the contract was not renewed by the Soviets.

The Central Selling Organization, however, does not handle about twenty percent of the world's diamonds, the majority of which comes from Ghana. In that country, a government Diamond Marketing Board grades, values, and prices rough diamonds and sells them to licensed buyers. Most of the product consists of industrial stones.

A portion of the supply from the Sierra Leone Selection Trust goes to specified buyers directly, with individual diggers and small mining operations in South Africa, South West Africa, and Lesotho selling to licensed buyers. Also, outside the CSO jurisdiction, are markets in the Central African Republic, the Ivory Coast, Guinea, and the South American states of Guyana, Venezuela, and Brazil, as well as the small production from India.

There are no quota arrangements for industrial diamonds. Instead, these are purchased by the Diamond Corporation from South Africa and other production operations and marketed through Industrial Distributors Limited, a sales branch of an organization of the same name.

Stones that are marketed in this manner are rough crystals. From the syndicated organizations, they go to jewelry manufacturers or company designers, then into the retail trade, and finally to the public.

CHAPTER 8

Industrial Diamonds

WHEN PARCELS OF STONES come from the mines in the Republic of South Africa and South West Africa, they are cleaned in acid, weighed, and counted. Then they are sorted into broad gem categories and also into diamonds suitable for industrial use only.

Since diamonds usually are considered gems, there is a tendency to think of industrial diamonds as the "trash of the trade." Although it is true that industrial diamonds are not suitable as gems because of awkward shapes, twinnings, bad coloring, or quality, their importance to industry cannot be underestimated. Prior to World War II, about seventy-five thousand carats of industrial diamonds were consumed by world industry. In 1966, that requirement had increased to at least thirty-two million carats and, projecting into the future, their use will rise annually at the rate of ten percent.

During the sorting process of African diamonds, which takes place at offices in Johannesburg, there is a grouping of diamond classified as "near gems." These are diamonds which are sold to Industrial Distributors in London and wind up as top industrial grades. Occasionally, the "near gems" will go into the gem markets, but this will depend on the demand and the prices being offered.

The most common industrial use for diamonds is the diamond core drill. This is a device which is capable of drilling through solid rock; it is constructed in such a manner that it will bring to the surface a continuous cylindrical rock core. This material can then be examined by geologists in their search for new ore deposits, testing the foundations of bridges and dams, and in the discovery of oil deposits.

To manufacture a diamond core drill, individual diamonds of one or two carats are set in the rim of a drill shaped in the form of a tube. As the drill is drawn out of a hole, after boring into a rock substance, for example, it brings with it the material into which the bore was made.

Another industrial use for the diamond involves permeating the edges of cutting tools and the surfaces of grinding wheels with diamonds tailored to the demand.

At first, industry did not consider the shape of the diamond particles to be important when used in grinding or cutting, but research has found that especially strong, "blocky" particles of diamond are needed for the demanding process of sawing and grinding. Impact crushers have been designed to produce a grit of special proportions needed for maximum operation of the tools.

A premium grade grit was developed which was used to produce a "metal bond," or the actual infusing of the grit into the metal. The grit is polished lightly to avoid fracturing the diamond particles in the sharpened edges of the saw operating at high speeds. To bond the grit to the metal, a resin is sometimes used first to retain the diamond particles. Then the resin is applied to the metal. In other instances, the grit is bonded directly to the metal. The procedure is still being researched, for sometimes resin works better than other times. Synthetic diamonds work best in resin bonds.

Before the laboratory developed the ideal drilling diamond stone, diamond drillers employed a technique peculiar to the trade in order to determine which stones were best suited for drilling purposes. The technique was to take the parcel of stones under consideration and simply tilt them. Those stones that rolled were kept for the drill, those that did not were rejected. Scientists have determined that the smooth, rounded diamonds, called "hardcore," are best for drilling. One reason for this is the tendency of rough crystals to fracture along a cleavage when placed under the extremes of pressure necessary for industrial use. So once the rougher stones are eliminated, the rest are placed in a centrifugal mill and polished to a high surface gloss, then metallically bonded to the drill.

Again, the toughness of diamond can be demonstrated graphically through industrial use. The hardest steel edge known will cut a five-mile groove in ordinary bronze before it must be sharpened. A tool made of tungsten carbide does not need sharpening until it has traveled twenty-one miles through the same material. But a tool cutting with a diamond edge can cut an unbelievable 1,200 miles through bronze.

The contemporary metals are made of tremendously hard materials, and diamond tools are the only devices suitable for industry. An example is the cutting of spaceship components made of very tough ceramics. Diamonds are the only material suitable here for cutting purposes.

Diamond tools have many various uses. Mass production factories such as those manufacturing components for automobile engines, make extensive use of diamond grinding techniques. Their abrasive grinding wheels are capable of maintaining tolerances of 0.001 of an inch or less; these must be periodically dressed with a diamond tool to shape the wheel, remove clogged or dull surfaces, and expose a new cutting edge.

When a modern highway is under construction, it is laid with a continuous strip of concrete. Expansion-contraction joints are later sawed into the surface using diamond grit on the saw blades. A machine with multiple diamond blades known as a "bump cutter," is used to cut runways at airports down to the required levels of uniformity necessary to safely land jet planes.

Diamond saws are used to cut through two-feet thick concrete walls; a diamond-impregnated blade on a thirty-inch diameter saw rotating at ninety miles per hour will take ten minutes to make a three-inch cut two and a half feet long in a piece of granite; saws with diamond edges are as broad as seventy-two inches so they can cut through marble; small natural diamonds are used in the burrs of a dentist's drill; a grinding head containing diamond segments is used to polish slabs of marble in a finishing shop in Vermont; to construct the city hall in Toronto, Canada, locking grooves were sawed into the marble used for facing strips. A twin-blade diamond saw specially made for the job sawed 1.3 million strips, or about three hundred miles of grooving.

The industrial use of diamonds has its delicate side in addition to the spectacular. Another well-known aspect of diamond tooling is the manufacture of record needles known as "styli." Most of the recorded music played throughout the world today uses diamond styli. This is precision material. The rough diamonds used are very small crystals which weigh a mere 1/400 of a carat each. First they are shaped into the form of a long, narrow box with one end rounded to a top-shaped tip. The tip radius of a stylus for playing stereo records is 8/10,000 of an inch.

As indicated above, diamonds have been used in space age technology. The diamond is capable of producing the very tight tolerances necessary for critical surface finishes needed to manufacture ultrasonic speed airplanes and some spaceships. The now familiar heat shield used to protect astronauts when they reenter the earth's atmosphere from outer space is shaped into a curved form on a lathe which uses a diamond tool.

A small but spectacular use of diamond is in the infrared detector, an instrument so sensitive that it can record the heat of a burning candle three miles away. The detector has a window made of a type of diamond so rare that it appears in one out of every thousand diamonds mined.

The synthetic jewel bearings used in control instruments in spaceships employ diamond in the manufacturing process.

Even false teeth now contain diamond dust to make them last longer and function with greater sharpness!

CHAPTER 9

Synthetic Diamonds

IN ORDER TO MAKE A DIAMOND, the same two components present in the earth when natural diamonds are formed must be present artificially: heat and pressure, both to extreme degrees.

Pure diamond will disintegrate in a vacuum, or an environment lacking oxygen. Between 800-1700 degrees Centigrade, a thin layer of the surface of diamond will be affected. But when the temperature reaches 1700 degrees, conversion to graphite takes place rapidly and thoroughly. Eventually, only a pile of graphite powder remains.

There is a startling similarity between crystalline carbon as graphite and the same substance as diamond. But changing the stable graphite into unstable diamond is a process which has proven to be anything but simple. The problem is to compress the hexagonal structure of carbon rings until the atoms become smaller cubic structures which characterize diamond. Also, the situation is complicated because when the pressure is removed, the atoms tend to spring back to their graphite structure. Heat is the agent which helps squeeze the atoms sufficiently and get them moving in the shape of the new diamond bonds.

In 1878, the first research of any importance in the synthesis of diamonds took place in Glasgow, Scotland. James Ballantyne Hannay, a Scottish chemist, conducted a series of about eighty experiments, three of which successfully produced diamonds. Hannay had been experimenting to find a solvent for alkali metals such as sodium and potassium, when he found that an inert substance such as paraffin would decompose when heated under pressure with hydrogen gas and one of the alkali metals. The carbon from the paraffin was freed when the hydrogen combined with the metal. This sparked the idea that carbon could be recrystallized as diamond.

Thick coils of wrought iron were created to contain the intense pressure needed. A tube, open at one end, was filled with the reaction material and sealed with a blacksmith's weld, then placed in a large reverbatory furnace for several hours. The mixture was ten percent bone oil and ninety percent paraffin to which metallic lithium had been added. After fourteen hours in the makeshift apparatus, the hard black mass lining three of the pipes yielded transparent crystals which proved to be diamond. Hannay sent about twelve of these particles to M. H. Story-Masklyne, who was then Keeper of Minerals in the British Museum. Story-Masklyne determined them to be diamonds. In 1943, the same particles were examined by X-ray, and eleven of the twelve particles proved to be diamond.

But Hannay's success was not sustained. In most of the eighty experiments which were unproductive, the tubes, exploded or leaked, or the furnace was wrecked. Although the materials he produced continue to exist, attempts to repeat the performance have not been successful.

Next came Henri Moissan, Professor of Mineralogical Chemistry in Paris, who conducted a lengthy series of experiments in which he attempted to select a metal that would expand on solidification, form an outer skin as it cooled, and thereby produce high pressures at the center. His theory was that this process should produce sufficient heat and pressure to form carbon into diamond. In 1904, he announced he had successfully produced diamonds by placing a crucible of pure carbon and iron in an electric furnace, then subjecting the mixture under extreme heat to great pressure by quickly cooling it. It is not known for sure whether Moissan actually produced diamonds, since the crystals he formed have not been found. The way in which he cooled the mixture was to take the molten mass of iron and carbon and plunge it into water to form a crust, then cool it in the air. Later, he found that by placing the mixture into molten lead, he could cool his substance more effectively. Then the entire result was solidified and placed in an acid bath. When the acid had done its work, the crystals were left which Moissan said were diamonds. The basis he used for his conclusion was that the particles would scratch ruby and, under microscopic examination and by measuring the amount of carbon dioxide produced when they were burned in oxygen, they tested out as diamond.

It is more likely that Moissan's product was silicon carbide or alumina. In more recent years. Moissan's work has been duplicated according to his own instructions, with about twenty crystals being produced. There was a certain similarity between these crystals and Moissan's published drawings when the crystals were examined by microscope. But when X-rayed, the crystals turned out to be silicon carbide, amorphous material, or alumina.

It was unfortunate that early synthetic diamond manufacturing leaned toward the goal of making gem diamonds.

Now this area of manufacturing is geared toward industrial diamond usage; it is here that synthetics have found their place of value.

One such success which fell short of its mark was made in 1953 by the Swedish firm known as Allmana Avenska, Elektriska Aktiebolaget, or ASEA. Their technique used pressure from 80,000-90,000 atmospheres at a maximum temperature of about 2760 degrees Centigrade. There is a problem maintaining such pressure, since the material with the highest compressive strength—carboloy—which is tungsten carbide cemented with cobalt, fails around 65,000 atmospheres. However, if the vessel used is shored by massive supports, pressures far beyond the yield point can be maintained. These supports are, in themselves, a rather complicated arrangement of six four-sided pyramids arranged with the points together to form a cube. Pressure is applied to the pyramids by six pistons and the assembly is placed in a tube about twenty-two inches in diameter, banded by steel. Into this is placed a hollow sphere of soapstone with thermite, and inside this another hollow sphere of tantalum. In the center of this second sphere is a reagent composed of iron carbide and graphite.

After being cooled and cut in half, diamonds were found in the center of the iron carbide. A factory had been established at Robertfors, in the northern portion of Sweden, and by 1964, industrial diamonds were being manufactured at a rate of about two million carats a year.

Although the Swedish experiments were successful in 1953, the preoccupation with producing gem diamonds delayed an announcement of the breakthrough until 1955. By then, success also had been achieved in American experiments.

The announcement of the American success came on February 15, 1953, when General Electric announced diamond had been manufactured at the GE laboratory in Schenectady, New York. During the experimental process, GE used a giant press to form the first crystals. A special pressure vessel in the large machine made it possible to create and maintain temperatures of 5000 degrees Farenheit and pressures of up to 2.4 million pounds per square inch, matching those conditions which existed 250 miles into the earth's crust. After four years of research, the General Electric press produced diamonds weighing only 1/100 of a carat. But they were diamonds. And the process could be repeated. GE applied for and obtained world patents to their process, totally unaware that ASEA also had a workable means of diamond production. However, the secrecy with which ASEA had conducted their work proved to be an advantage for General Electric.

There were meaningful differences between the American and Swedish methods. GE had discovered that pyrophyllite, a soft, slate-like material, had a unique property conducive to synthetic diamonds. That property is hydrous aluminum silicate which originates in the same mineral family as the material used in slate pencils, talc, and as the steatite or soapstone used in the Swedish process. When subjected to pressures of extreme proportions, the melting point of hydrous aluminum silicates rises from 2400 degrees F to 4800 degrees F, or 2720 degrees C.

A ring of tungsten carbide is a strategic part of the General Electric method, for it comprises the "belt," which is both versatile and tough. A hole in the center is shaped into a cylinder, flared at each end. Two tapered pistons drive in opposite ends of the central hole and pressure is applied to the pistons by a large hydraulic press.

Diamond is manufactured by filling a short cylinder of pyrophyllite with graphite or another form of carbon, along with tantalum or nickel. This reaction material is placed into the hole in the center of the belt. Pressure is applied, and a current of electricity is passed through the center to run up the temperature. The pyrophyllite becomes a type of gasket which seals any gaps and flows under extreme pressure, allowing the pistons to advance and compress the carbon and metal.

Additionally, the pyrophyllite acts to prevent leakage of the electric current and the heat when the current is passed through. Pressures of more than 100,000 atmospheres, or about 1.5 million pounds per square inch, are achieved, along with temperatures above 2000 degrees C.

The diamonds are recovered by administering acid to the hard black mass which results, and retrieving the crystals which are left behind.

Within a month of the General Electric announcement, a decision was made to research a commercial process for making diamond at De Beers Consolidated Mines. Working in cooperation with the Belgian Congo mining company— the Societe Miniere du Beceka—the process was announced in 1959 as a success.

A South African process also employed a belt system.

A patent dispute developed between General Electric and De Beers, but it was settled to the satisfaction of both.

Seventy-five high voltage presses are used in Ultra High Pressure Units in Springs, an area near Johannesburg. The process uses pyrophyllite cylinders with tapered rings over each end, and a reaction material of discs made of carbon and nickel. The operating cycle is only two or three minutes.

World production of synthetics in 1969 was estimated at forty million carats, compared with forty-four million carats of natural diamonds. The process of manufacturing synthetic diamonds has come a long way in a short time, and it now ranks as a common procedure.

Synthetic diamonds usually are small and not of gem

quality. Mostly they are used as abrasive grit in resinoid-bonded grinding wheels. Research is continuing in the production of larger industrial stones, but so far, the primary use is in abrasive grit.

There are political considerations in the manufacturing of synthetic diamonds. The major producer of the natural diamond crystal is the Congo, whose history as a political nation is unstable. Since the diamond is so strategic in the manufacture of certain defense weapons and in space technology, the manufacturing process in America (and the entire western world) has been especially meaningful; it has afforded independence from the importation of natural diamon grit, or bort.

A relatively new process, developed by General Electric, was announced three years ago. Clear, white synthetic gem quality diamonds were produced in a laboratory. Some of the crystals manufactured weighed more than a carat, but they cost considerably more to produce than the natural gem quality rough from Africa.

The process also involves the belt-type system using a special pressure chamber. A small mass of synthetic diamond crystals is placed in the center of the chamber and on each side a bath of iron or nickel is produced. The synthetic diamonds form seed crystals. The catalyst metal (iron or nickel) becomes molten during operation, freeing carbon atoms in the bath. A higher temperature is maintained in the center of the chamber than at the ends, thereby allowing more carbon to dissolve at the center than at the cooler ends. However, the carbon atoms come out of solution at the center and crystallize at the ends. Normally they would crystallize as graphite, but the seed crystals at each end attract the carbon atoms which attach to the seeds until the mass is consumed by the seeds. The greater the difference in temperature from the center to the ends of the chamber, the faster the seed crystals grow.

Temperatures are held for several days at pressures approaching 60,000 atmospheres. Impurities can be added to the process to provide such features as color, electrical properties, hardness, internal structure, and other characteristics of gem diamonds.

There is more regularity to diamonds produced synthetically than those found in mines. The irregularities in the naturals probably are the result of rocks compressing around the diamonds as they formed.

When the lowest possible range of temperatures and pressures is applied in the synthetic process, the crystals grow in cubes. The layers begin in the center of the faces and grow outward so that each face is smooth, whereas the surface of natural cubes are rough and pitted.

Octahedra form at higher temperatures and pressures. If the higher temperatures and pressures are maintained, though, the crystal will grow to a certain size, then begin to dissolve.

Although diamond crystals grow quickly in belt system production (about a third of a millimeter per second), better quality crystals result from a slower growth cycle.

Currently, research is centered on producing sufficiently large crystals for use in tools and drills crowns as well as for application in electronics.

The Retailing of Diamonds

THE SALE OF GEMSTONES (minerals or other natural material having the necessary beauty and durability for use as jewelry) now grosses some one billion dollars a year in the United States alone. Such sales include not only diamond, but opal, emerald, jade, sapphire, and ruby.

But this figure means little unless a jewelry store owner or manager believes he is taking a fair cut of that annual one billion dollars. It's one thing to have sufficient product knowledge so the retailer can share his knowledge with any customer who happens to enjoy hearing about gems. However, unless that type of customer comes into the store, that knowledge is going to remain a rather private privilege of the personnel.

Everything that has gone into this study of diamonds so far—every word, phrase, fact, and legend—is of great use to those people interested in diamonds.

There are four basic concepts that must be considered in

bringing a diamond from the ground to a jewelry store: market, promotion, traffic, and sales.

Few women in the world would refuse to own and wear diamonds. In other words, nearly every woman alive wants to own and wear at least one diamond. She's just waiting for her chance—whether it comes in the form of an engagement ring, a special birthday, the day her husband gets that sought-after raise, or when she and her husband feel they've reached the point where jewelry can become a more integral part of their lives together.

Before selling to an individual, the retailer must be aware of what his customer can afford to pay. He must know the economics of the area in which his store is located. In a large city's numerous economic areas, as well as in the smaller cities and towns throughout the nation, there exists six basic marketing groups to which a promotional program can be aimed. Knowing the economic groups which exist within the reach of the retailer's store is basic to the approach he must take in order to capitalize on that market.

The six groups that exist within nearly every market are the wealthy, the professionals, middle management, white collar, blue collar, and students. There is market potential within every one of these groups. The retailer must know the population distribution of these groups within his marketing area, and the buying habits of each.

In large cities, wealthy people predominate more than they do in smaller cities or towns. An exclusive group of customers are an asset to any jewelry store. But it is necessary to know how many exclusive groups there are, and what their buying habits may be. This means that the retailer must know if these people are conservative or if they tend to follow trends in styling; do they tend to shop at local jewelry stores or buy in other cities or countries?

Most wealthy people are not interested in the spectacular. Rather, they appreciate quality and service. They can be an asset to any store operation since they are fairly regular in their diamond buying habits. They also influence to some extent, at least two of the other marketing groups in following their purchasing habits—professionals and middle management. These are the people who believe they will be among the wealthy some day and are working toward that goal.

Professionals include the top executives in business, attorneys, doctors, top-level government and political people, and generally people who have achieved affluence and are prepared to spend it for their own personal comfort and betterment.

Like the wealthy, they appreciate quality, but occasionally they will be attracted by the spectacular. Also, they are mobile to some extent, moving from one community to another as they advance within their profession. Therefore, it is important for the retailer to know when such people move into his marketing area.

Middle management personnel are the young people on their way up; they will become the top executives, the most influential lawyers and doctors and educators in the future years. They have more than adequate incomes, but they also are rearing families and have expenses common to the growing family. They enjoy good jewelry, but appreciate pieces which can be adapted for different occasions. Also, they are group-oriented; sell one and you probably will sell others in the same social or professional group.

With the growing affluence within social America since World War II, there has been a blending of white and blue collar workers. There is little economic distinction between the two groups. These are people who make good money, but their struggle with monthly expenses take up most of their income, especially if they are trying to fit into a social grouping somewhat beyond their means. They include truck drivers and bricklayers, junior executives, and generally those within the $10,000-$20,000 a year income group, depending on the area of the country. They are turned off by a retailer who usually appeals to the wealthy or top professionals. They are turned off by too much of the spectacular, but they remain a potent part of every community and certainly have the buying power to help make a profit and loss statement more appealing at the end of the year. Communicating with this type of individual is vital to the successful sale of jewelry.

College communities can be viable markets for jewelry stores. Again, it is a matter of communicating. Students and young people below the age of twenty-five believe they are pacesetters. They pattern their lifestyles after hero images of their generation. Knowing these popular images and understanding them will make it possible for a retailer's merchandise to appeal to the young—even the diamonds. They find excitement in shopping but not necessarily in buying; they enjoy action and new things. Style is very important to them, even if that style might appear to be somewhat shabby when compared with styles a generation or two ago. Most of them have money to spend and the appeal made to their interests determines where and how they spend it.

The way to identify these groups and their influence on the community or marketing area is through personal knowledge. And this knowledge is relatively simple to gain. A daily newspaper is crammed with the activities of each of these groups. It is inconceivable to think that a retailer who wants to increase sales would not read at least one daily newspaper—preferably the one printed in the immediate area served by the store. On the front page are the faces and names of the people who make news because they are intelligent, active, and innovative; on the society pages are the pictures and stories of the families of many of these same people; on the sports pages are the pictures and stories of their children and a reflection of their popularity in the community; on the financial pages are the stories of their exploits.

Knowing who they are and keeping a list of their names and addresses—even a picture or two—is one good way of finding them when you have something you think they may want. When you know the people, you can contact them. If a special article appears complimenting something they have accomplished, a mailing piece enclosing the article in an attractive card with the name of your store on it, indicates your interest, not just in their money but in the accomplishment.

The Chamber of Commerce in each community maintains listings of economic activity and statistical data which is very useful in marketing. Every year there are studies of some type which are issued by government or civic agencies; these indicate something more about the nature of the potential market. Every ten years, this country conducts a census which reflects far more than just how many people happen to live in a particular city or town. This is public record and available to anyone who wishes to determine more precisely the economic health of a particular area.

More knowledge about the area in which a particular store is located means more knowledge about its people. That kind of knowledge almost automatically ignites ideas for marketing which can increase store traffic.

Once a market breakdown is acquired, it is necessary to decide on a promotional approach in order to attract the various human elements within that market. This involves two considerations which are vital to success: communication and image. You may communicate your message with accuracy and appeal; but if your store image discourages a customer when he responds to that appeal, you've probably lost him as a customer. If your store image is precise and accurately reflects the market, but you fail to communicate the message, there will be no increase in sales. Therefore, the two are intertwined and must be coordinated to produce the best results.

When building store image, the retailer must keep in mind that he is dealing with more than one market. If his market potential includes only two percent of the population which can be classified as "wealthy," it does little good to appeal only to that negligible percentage of the market. Also, if fifty percent of the market is among the white and blue collar group, you cannot build an image of blatant affluence or one of grocery store garishness and expect to appeal to the customer.

Unless an unusually large portion of the market falls into one particular income group, you probably will have to strike a medium somewhere between an appeal to professional and lower income groups. This involves creating an image which combines elegance with warmth and allows members of both income groups to feel welcome and comfortable in the atmosphere of the store once they enter the front door.

People enjoy touching what they might buy. This is not to say a jewelry store must openly display all diamonds, but a customer should be allowed to handle the jewelry if he desires, in the company of a sales person.

In-store atmosphere is another important consideration in retailing diamonds. It is necessary to remember the significance of diamonds. They are at once things of love, beauty, status, value, and fashion. No other product can lay claim to as many attributes as a diamond possesses. If these attributes are all subliminal parts of in-store atmosphere, an appeal to almost every potential buyer will be realized.

Promoting the image you desire calls for a specific type of advertising. Advertising is nothing more than *appealing communication*. But those two words, "appeal" and "communication," must receive equal consideration in an advertising program.

A general rule for budgeting in this area is to allow about five percent of gross annual income for this purpose. Then the amount of revenue this generates for advertising must be broken down into the media available to promote the retailing program. There are no hard and fast rules for using the various media, although certain media draw better attraction than others on a nationwide basis. Whatever works best in the individual jewelry store deserves the lion's portion of the advertising budget.

The most common media available include newspaper, radio, television, direct mail, and window displays, not necessarily in that order. The main point to remember in deciding on budget proportions for the various media is that each media representative who calls on your store should have at his disposal information on which to base the projected success of a particular promotional program. If the advertising representative does not have this information, it is doubtful that he is taking his job seriously enough to warrant your hard-earned cash. So don't be afraid to ask questions of the advertising man. Newspapers, radio stations, and television stations all assign certain retailers to certain ad salespeople. It is then the job of these salespeople to call on you regularly, not just to sell you advertising, but to service your account as well. These individuals should be a good source of marketing information. If they know their job, they too have studied the markets which exist in the community and can help you plan an effective program.

Circulation figures don't tell you all there is to know about a newspaper's potential to sell your product. It certainly is necessary to know the certified number of households the newspaper reaches. But it is also important to know the success or lack of success on the part of advertisers in that newspaper who sell products comparable in price to your own, such as the more exclusive clothing store, furriers, or automobile dealers. If you've seen an ad in the newspaper which seemed likely to pull in store traffic for sale of mink coats, find out whether or not the store manager credits that ad with the sales that followed.

Find out if the newspaper is read by the people who subscribe to it; learn if it is *respected* as a newspaper or *tolerated* as a necessary part of the community. A newspaper that lies at the front door or is thrown away after the comics are read is not going to sell your product.

It is likely that more than one radio or television station is available. Who are the listening audiences of each? Find out what time of day your ads will be heard or viewed. It isn't always possible to get prime time spots.

Listen carefully to what the media advertising representative suggests as a possible promotional program for your store. This individual has been trained to know a market and appeal to it. Also, he has at his disposal several marketing guides which include successful programs in other communities comparable to your own. Find out what these are and if they can be adapted to your personal needs.

Never discount the potential power of an advertising dollar if it is spent wisely. It is one of the biggest businesses in the world today and there has to be a reason for that. The reason is that the people who take the best advantage of the potential, realize increased sales and profits.

Direct mailing should be reserved for special occasions. This can become a most expensive way of promotion if the retailer is not careful. It should be reserved for special events and used to supplement the regular method of advertising (newspaper, radio, television). Here again there are guidelines in the form of preprinted advertisements which can be adapted to your needs. As a retailer, you probably have received some in the mail already. Don't throw them all away. Save the ones you feel might serve some purpose at a later date and file them in your advertising file.

Direct mailings as supplemental promotions are most successful with special events, such as reopening after a remodeling, the arrival of a special shipment of gems, perhaps the loan of a unique precious stone which can be used for display purposes, or a special calendar day (Mother's Day, Valentine's Day, etc.).

Keep in mind that direct mailings will not be read by a number of the household unless the first thing that the individual sees captures his interest sufficiently to warrant further reading. This is true of all advertising whether it's print or audio-visual. Interest must be captured immediately in order to hold attention. This is especially true in direct mailings since the person who receives the flyer can easily put it aside or throw it away without even a glance. If you are able to get ten percent of the readers inside the brochure you can consider your mailing a success. This means that if you mail five thousand pieces and five hundred of them are read, and ten percent of that number actually become store traffic, you have fifty customers to sell. Since you're selling diamonds, if you complete a sale to five of those fifty, you've probably paid for the mailing and made a profit as well.

Display windows are the most readily available means of advertising and can be the most effective, or, for that matter, the least effective. Here you must depend on your own imagination. There is no doubt that potential store traffic is stopped by a display in a jewelry-store window. Especially in the more tradition-minded communities, it is common to find young couples standing in front of a diamond ring display, obviously trying to decide which piece the young woman desires most as an engagement ring.

More and more retail stores are going for selectivity in window displays rather than a little bit of everything. This selectivity must be combined with some imagination in order to change a potential customer into a satisfied buyer.

For example, an interesting display could include not only gems, but the equipment a jeweler uses to set and repair gemstones. It doesn't have to be extensive to be interesting. But since most people do not even have a passing knowledge of the equipment used by a jeweler, such a display, combined with the gems, can produce in-store traffic. Mineral samples and rough crystals can also be used in window displays as long as some imagination and display creativity are part of the process.

Always keep at least two current subscriptions going to house organs which provide ideas and methods of promotion. These magazines are published by experts in the field of diamond promotion, and they share with their readers the successful promotion programs of jewelers throughout the world. Many of the ideas can be tailored to your local store needs.

Another form of promotion might be a diamond party which includes select customers as guests. It might be a cocktail affair in the early evening, an afternoon coffee for wives, or a full-scale evening showing complete with short lectures, drinks, and hors d'oeuvres.

If you happen to be a person who enjoys speaking to groups, here is an especially potent promotional device. Every community has high schools, civic clubs, and women's groups which are always looking for speakers. By taking your product knowledge, constructing some portable displays, and working up an interesting address, you can promote your store without ever mentioning the name. On the other hand, be sure your approach conforms to the audience; a group of businessmen are not going to be interested in the same information and approach as a group of society women. The men may be fascinated by the technology involved in mining, finishing, and retailing, while the women will be intrigued with the finished product and its characteristics.

Through a combination of the promotional concepts here presented, increased store traffic will certainly result. But promotion does not mean sales. Sales are completed in the store and depend on the approach made when a sales person meets the customer.

Every diamond purchase is an important event to the customer. More than likely it is going to take more money than he ordinarily would like to spend on a piece of jewelry which is worn for beauty rather than utility. Utility, of course, is a part of a diamond's existence, since its durability extends far beyond the life of the original purchaser. It also has a value which does not diminish.

Since the potential purchaser, while looking at the gem, is analyzing its cost in his mind, he must be treated as an individual with individual needs and desires. Most customers want to take their time deciding on a diamond purchase. It's an important decision to them and if they feel hurried they can easily go to another store where someone else will take the necessary time to meet their emotional as well as economic needs.

Buying a diamond is unlike any other purchase. In the customer's mind there are thoughts which combine romance, economics, information, and uncertainty. The secret of selling is to determine the extent of each of these thoughts of the customer and appeal to them reasonably and adequately. The jeweler will almost always close a sale as a result.

The truth is that a diamond is as natural as the love one person has for another. Without becoming maudlin about it, the retailer, when making a sale, can include the story of diamond woven into the fabric of romance that makes the two inseparable. The qualities of durability, brilliance, fire, and sheer beauty are some of the considerations in such an approach.

When a diamond is purchased as an engagement ring, however small the gem might be, this does not necessarily mean the end of that customer's relationship with the retailer. It could be the beginning of a long relationship, especially if the young couple making the initial purchase remains in the community for several years. As income increases, they will be back to make additional purchases according to their fashion needs. They will return to the jewelry store where they feel most welcome and where they feel they have been honestly received and treated as individuals, not just as part of general store traffic.

Index

Italic figures denote illustrations